HERRIOT
A Vet's Life

W.R.Mitchell

GREAT NORTHERN

Great Northern Books
PO Box 213, Ilkley, LS29 9WS
www.greatnorthernbooks.co.uk

Every effort has been made to acknowledge correctly and contact the copyright holders of material in this book. Great Northern Books Ltd apologises for any unintentional errors or omissions, which should be notified to the publisher.

ISBN: 978 1 905080 77 9

Design and layout: David Burrill

CIP Data
A catalogue for this book is available from the British Library

Contents

Alf Wight – much better known as James Herriot – on a farm visit. (Paul S Conklin)

Quoting Alf Wight

The high country is too bleak for some people, but it is up there on the empty moors, with the curlews crying, that I have been able to find peace and tranquillity of mind.

I am never at my best in the early morning, especially a cold morning in the Yorkshire spring, with a piercing March wind sweeping down from the fells, finding its way inside my clothing, nipping at my nose and ears.

Those who have read my books will know that behind everything I have written, funny and serious, has been the glorious backcloth of the Yorkshire countryside.

About this Book ....

Bill Mitchell was recently voted the Dales National Park's greatest living cultural icon. Polling was a feature of each National Park to mark their 60th anniversary. In the Dales, Alf Wight – much better known as James Herriot, a celebrated vet, won the main accolade as an icon who had died but was still revered.

In this book, the two are re-united, with Bill Mitchell as the author and Alf as the main character, along with his son Jim, a vet who often accompanied him on his rounds. Both applied their veterinary skills to ailing farmstock and household pets in the Pennine dales and across the North East Moors.

Bill Mitchell gathered much of his information from interviews with father and son. Jim kindly allowed him to quote a few passages from his authorised biography of his father. In compiling this book, Bill could not resist adding Herriot-like tales of Dales characters he met as a long-time Editor of *The Dalesman*, in a characterful period overlapping that known to Alf, who courted and wed a local lass. Bill was married to Freda, a Yorkshire farmer's daughter, for 55 years.

FOREWORD – 1

by Christopher Timothy

The day I learned I had landed the role of James Herriot my excitement was indescribable and I immediately rang Bill Sellars the producer. There were a few weeks before filming commenced and I really wanted to meet the man himself. "Please?" Bill said that wasn't a good idea. He explained that Alf Wight was a very private retiring man who fights shy of publicity and anything "showbizzy". I pleaded and was dissuaded.

In the books he describes his family, colleagues, patients and their owners in great entertaining detail and little or nothing of himself. I did what research I could. Two things I knew for sure – he didn't smoke and never wore a hat. Not much to go on!

We met about two weeks into filming the first series in 1977. Alf was shy and diffident and he obviously enjoyed his success but was not over enamoured of the attendant fuss and to-do. He was everything one gleams from the books and a lot more. Apart from being a consummate storyteller he was kind and compassionate – a genuine animal lover and a people lover too!

He had boundless energy, he was learned, and he was humble and with a great sense of humour and the ridiculous, his undisputed talent as a writer equalled by his obvious ability as a vet. I have never heard an ill word of him. He was loved and admired and I loved and admired him too. What an incredible legacy he left. I miss him very much and my life has been all the better for knowing him.

Christopher Timothy
June 2010

FOREWORD – 2

by Jim Wight

Young veterinary surgeon Alf Wight and his client, Tommy Cooper, stood forlornly over the old recumbent cow. Despite Alf's utmost efforts to revive her over the previous week, both men knew that the poor animal's days were numbered.

'I'm afraid the only course of action is to send the old girl in for humane slaughter, Mr Cooper,' he said, quietly. 'She's beginning to suffer now.'

Alf thought for a moment before conveying some more unwelcome news for the farmer.

'She's so thin, Mr Cooper. All skin and bone. I doubt whether she'll pass as fit for human consumption.'

The old man took the bad tidings philosophically. In those days, the loss of an animal could be tempered somewhat with a financial payment for the meat following certification from the veterinary surgeon that the animal was not suffering from a condition hazardous to human health.

'Aye, ah doubt thou's reet,' he said with a slow shake of the head. 'She's ower brust ter mak owt on!'

Having worked for over a decade among Yorkshire farmers, Alf understood that barrage of old Yorkshire dialect, but during his first early years in Thirsk it would have been akin to a foreign language.

He had been brought up as a city boy on the streets of Glasgow, and from his first tentative days as a green young veterinary surgeon in the Yorkshire market town of Thirsk, he had been intrigued by a way of life so different from his own – a life of hard work and Spartan existence, all carried out with a fundamental honesty and philosophical outlook. 'Only them as 'as 'em lose 'em' was something he heard countless times while staring gloomily at one of his less successful cases laid out on a cow byre floor.

Another quality of some of the old Yorkshiremen, an inborn reluctance to part with their money, was a problem that Alf Wight had to grapple with for a large part of his professional life, but his experiences with the farmers and their 'vet bills' were well remembered and put down on paper to good effect in the future.

As a vet he was especially interested in their quirky old remedies for ailing stock, and this fascination with all these aspects of Yorkshire country life was to result, years later, in his writing world best-selling books under the pseudonym of James Herriot.

The dry humour of the old countryman was never lost on Alf. As a great observer of human nature he missed nothing and the Yorkshire humour strides across the pages of every Herriot book.

In 1995 – the year of his death – my sister and I took part in a television programme called 'Tracks', a series of favourite walks of well-known celebrities.

As one of James Herriot's favourites, we chose a walk from Keld in Swaledale, down the valley of the River Swale to the village of Muker. A helicopter was involved, to film our walk from above.

A local farmer from Keld was interested in the helicopter, and especially the cost of the hire.

'Ow much!' he exclaimed when told the price per hour of helicopter hire. He thought for a moment before continuing.

'Yer off int' 'elicopter down t' valley ter Muker are yer?'

'Yes,' I replied.

A smile crossed his face. 'Yer couldn't fit a sprayer under t' chopper could yer? Ah 'ave some bad bracken in yon valley needs sortin' out!' The future James Herriot had rich material for his books working with men like this in his early years in the Yorkshire Dales.

This lavishly illustrated book about James Herriot is one with a difference. As well as an account of the life of the world's most famous vet, Bill Mitchell gives a description of life in the northern moors and dales that the real James Herriot found so interesting. No one is better qualified to talk on this subject than Bill. He draws on a lifetime of experiences (among them, many years as editor of that eternally popular magazine *The Dalesman*), living with, interviewing and writing about Yorkshire people.

I feel privileged to have known two icons of Yorkshire, Alf White and Bill Mitchell, Alf as a great father, and Bill as one with whom I have talked several times about the fascinating characters who have crossed his path.

James Herriot's books are history; they describe a way of life for the countryman, farmer and veterinary surgeon that is fast disappearing. People are interested in history and this is one of the reasons for their enduring popularity.

This book, *Herriot – A Vet's Life*, is history too. Written by a man with unsurpassed knowledge and experience of Yorkshire country life, it is an evocative description of times gone by. Just as James Herriot has done, Bill Mitchell has preserved in print a part of our heritage that should never be forgotten. I wish this book every success.

Jim Wight
June 2010

1

AN AFTERNOON WITH ALF WIGHT

Having been invited to open a Dales craft-trail based on Thirsk, I wrote to Alf Wight, alias James Herriot. Might I "pop in" to see him? He replied by phone in a gentle voice that had a faint Glaswegian inflection from his upbringing in that city. Said Alf: "I think I owe you a favour."

With a light heart, and the Herriot television jingle in my mind, I motored eastwards to Thirsk – to the Darrowby of the Herriot books, a composite town Alf described as "a bit of Thirsk, something of Richmond, Leyburn and Middleham, and a fair chunk of my imagination."

As usual when passing through the old market town, I called at South Villa for a special forecast from Bill Foggitt who, well into his eighties and almost blind, foretold the coming weather using natural signs – even midges - in favour of scientific instruments.

His first inclination when rising from his bed was to look across fields to the tower of the church. It was in clear view an hour or so before I arrived. Bill assured me that the day would be dry and sunny. He added a light-hearted note, a surprise from the lips of a Methodist local preacher: "When the townscape looks blurred, I can still fine-focus on a pint at the *Three Tuns.*"

I officially opened the craft-trail. Those who followed it through the dale-country would meet a variety of craftworkers in a glorious setting. Before meeting Alf, I briefly sampled Herriot Country from a viewpoint on Sutton Bank, at the rim of the Hambleton Hills. It was a view chosen for the cover of a picture book, *James Herriot's Yorkshire*, that sold millions of copies.

Walden, an off-shoot of Wensleydale well known to James Herriot.

Alf Wight receiving the Queen's Salver, awarded in recognition of services to the county and its people in 1983. The presentation is being made by the then Lord Mayor of Leeds, Councillor Martin Dodgson. (Yorkshire Post Newspapers)

Before me was a mist-wrapped Plain of York extending to a line of grey-blue Pennine fells. Jim, Alf's son, remarked about the photograph: "Dad faced the Pennines, which always meant most to him." Alf was in his 50s when he penned his first James Herriot book. This collection of tales looking back at a first year in practice, with dates and people's identity altered to avoid offending friends and clients, set the pattern for many books to come.

Herriot Country, his literary creation, was defined as "the area between two lines drawn from the heads of Coverdale and Swaledale, across the Plain of York and over the Hambleton Hills and the North York Moors to the lovely villages of the Coast." He allowed for "two bulges", for Harrogate and York, where he and his family spent many a half-day at leisure.

Alf penned many tales, some grave, some cheerful, but without extreme violence or sensuality. He added some refreshing dashes of humour. All is not lost when people laugh. The hero of the saga (if Alf Wight might thus be termed) rarely asserted himself. Early on in his books, he was both shy and diffident, a victim of practical jokes and embarrassing situations.

Swaledale was the most beautiful place he visited. When he tried to buy a local cottage he failed. In retrospect, it might have been a good thing. "Swaledale can be very busy at the week-ends." To lonesome Alf, it was thrilling to go up a little side valley like Walden, off-shoot of Wensleydale, and walk over the old road till he had a view of Carlton in Coverdale and Little Whernside.

In 1978, Alf bought a cottage at West Scrafton, Coverdale. He revelled in the charm of this isolated little valley, which became his Dales retreat, far from the Herriot "honeypots". When he set off walking, he invariably had a dog at foot. A Bradford lady who drove her father around the quieter dales, and asked him what he thought about them, had a terse reply: "It were nowt but scenery!"

Now I was making my first visit to Thirlby, the home of Alf, his wife Joan and Bodie, a Border terrier. Mirebeck, the last house in the village, reposed behind a tall hedge. They had secreted themselves away in this quiet spot in the spring of 1979, just ten years after Joan had urged Alf to submit the manuscript of his first Herriot book to a literary agent, who contacted Michael Joseph, the London publishers, and launched a busy Yorkshire vet on a highly-successful career as an author.

The workings of my tape-recorder were double-checked; it was about to capture the voice of an author who had become world-famous – as closely associated with the Yorkshire Dales as was Wordsworth with the Lake District and the Brontës with heather-thatched moors above Haworth.

Approaching the door of Mirebeck, I had a mental picture of part of the opening sequence of a cinema version of Alf's stories. Entitled *Creatures Great and Small*, it had James Herriot, newly qualified as a vet, ringing the doorbell of a veterinary surgery. A pack of noisy dogs bounced off the front door. Mrs Hall, housekeeper, restrained them before confronting James. So, pictorially, began the Herriot saga...

Alf, being alone in Mirebeck, responded to my knock on the door. The face and the quiet manner were familiar from his occasional appearances on television. As Editor of *The Dalesman*, I had read and reviewed Alf's books. When, in my daily work, I asked a Dales farmer about conditions in the 1930s, he had replied: "Tha mun read 'erriot." His friend had grinned and remarked: "Thou were lucky. In t'thirties I couldn't afford a vet."

Alf and his family had been ensconced in Thirsk when I wrote an article about the place for the *The Dalesman* in 1960. Unknown to me, the quiet, hard-working vet, about whom local people spoke with a sense of awe, was a worrier. He did not put his feelings on parade. Alf had just lost his father, known as Pop. He had little cash. His two children, Jim and Rosie, were entering the higher education zone. There were a few veterinary staff problems.

At Thirsk, a vet was not inclined to be run off his feet. The town stands at an altitude of 115 feet above sea level, in the gentle Vale of Mowbray, and local farmers were mainly arable men, growing almost anything you cared to mention, including sugar beet, potatoes, other root crops, and the usual run of cereals. Alf, sensing a gradual shrinking of pasturage, and therefore of farm stock, had periods of depression.

It surprised me to find that what appeared to be a single place was in two parishes. A local man snapped when I mentioned the name. He said: "Nay, tha's in Sowerby now. Thirsk is across yon street." The market place was broad; the inlets and outlets tended to be narrow, having a throttling effect on traffic at busy times, such as the holiday season and the days when horse-racing attracted excited hordes, the peak of patronage being on Ebor Day.

Benjamin Foggitt, chemist, related that on the market days of his youth the town attracted crowds of farm folk with dog-carts and masses of farm produce. Flocks of geese from Ireland, driven into the market place at the end of September, were bought for fattening on stubble for the Christmas market.

The only auction mart in town handled around 30 cattle, 200 sheep and 50 pigs a week, most of which were bought by butchers from Middlesbrough, Leeds, Bradford and York. Stock had a good reputation. Prices were equal, if not better, than at other markets in the area.

During a chat with a local farmer at a local cafe, I collected two amusing tales about food. At a big farm, the men knew when the farmer's wife was making jam roly poly pudding for dinner. She wore only one stocking! At another farm, the hired man, asked if he wanted an egg to eat for tea, replied: "I'm that hungry I could eat t'ruddy hen 'at laid it."

I wandered along Kirkgate and saw what looked like a mini-cathedral and was the parish church, St Mary's, being the centre of local spiritual life for 500 years. I heard it referred to as The Mother Church of Cleveland, with seating for about 500 people. Alf Wight married Joan

Danbury at this grand, red stone edifice.

I met the Wight family at a reception in a Leeds hotel in 1979. That evening saw the launch of the aforementioned book, *James Herriot's Yorkshire*, a hefty, well-illustrated tome that was virtually an afterthought but would break all records for sales.

I introduced myself to Donald, senior partner in the busy veterinary practice, and to Brian, his shorter, stockier brother. They appeared in the Herriot books under Wagnerian names – Siegfried and Tristan – and provided much of the action and many of the stories that Alf, a keen observer, occupying neutral ground, would readily acknowledge.

Alf, questioned about his use of the fictitious name Darrowby for Thirsk, in his first book – *If Only They Could Talk* - published in 1970, replied: "It has to be Thirsk. I was married here. My kids were born here. They went to school in Thirsk. I have put Darrowby in the books as a composite term. But really, Thirsk is Darrowby. It is a place of great charm. People who live here are lucky in that they can go west to the Dales or go east to the lovely Moors, contrasting types of scenery. There's a lovely feeling of freedom and spaciousness about this part of Yorkshire."

At that tucked-away village of Thirlby, I had a gracious welcome from Alf who, with Bodie at heel, led the way to his first-floor study. At the dawn of his writing career, he read a teach-yourself-to-write book. His first scribblings were made in the lounge of the modest family home at Thirsk. Alf had tapped the keys of a small typewriter for half an hour or so at the end of each busy day. Joan his wife would be busying herself with household jobs and television was invariably running its noisy course in a corner of the room.

In the big study where our chat – too informal to be classified as an interview – took place, there was a peaceful atmosphere. We talked quietly. My eyes occasionally strayed to a state-of-the-art computer. Alf reclined on a swivel chair. Bodie, almost the colour of a door-mat, lay between his legs and fixed me with an unblinking gaze. I was told that Bodie was eight and a-half years old. When I commented that it looked older, Alf remarked: "Border terriers go white very early. They look older than they really are."

To Jim Wight, Bodie was "self-willed" and "whiskery faced". Regarded as "a bit of a show-off", the dog posed appealingly for photography and had a tendency to display a haughty superiority over others of his kind. Bodie was antagonistic towards other male dogs, which is why Alf would slip a lead on to Bodie's collar when they were to go on a walk.

Alf accounted for the hint of Scottishness in his voice. He was born in Sunderland. At the age of three weeks, the family moved to Glasgow. This was his home for twenty-three years. "As a city boy, I grew up in a world of bustle and trams."

Glasgow is flanked by beautiful country. "I spent all my boyhood and youth on the Scottish mountains. We used to go camping nearly every week-end." Caught up in the Great Outdoors movement of the 1930s, "we saw hundreds of cyclists and walkers with packs on their backs...We went up to the Gairloch and looked over the 'Duke of Argyll's Bowling Green' to the 'Cobbler' and the great mountains."

When Alf qualified as a veterinary surgeon in 1939, few jobs were available. He spent a short time with Jock McDowell, a vet whose practice was based on Sunderland, being paid three guineas a week, a third of which he handed to an aunt who provided him with bed and breakfast. The job lasted for six months.

Alf then found employment at Thirsk, in the North Riding of Yorkshire. Alf was now based in a compact little town between the Pennines and the Moors, where several A- class roads converged, the church was like a mini-cathedral, there were two notable old inns and farmers thronged the place on market day, though most of the adjacent land was arable. "I think there was a chap called Hardwick who told somebody who told me about the job. So I dashed off to Thirsk and got the job – thank heavens!"

Alf Wight in his spacious study at Mirebeck, the last house in the village of Thirlby, near Thirsk.

Alf relaxes at home. His wife Joan had encouraged him in his writing career.

Opposite: Alf in the glorious countryside of the Yorkshire Dales above Arncliffe, with his son Jim (top), granddaughter Katrina and Bodie (bottom). (Jim Wight collection)

What did Alf think of the Dales when he first saw them? "They were much less dramatic than Scotland but they have a serenity about them – a personal beauty."

Alf, knowing little about Yorkshire, expected to find himself in a seedy, industrialised county. He was amazed at the grandeur of the Dales and Moors. The advertisement for the job stated "mainly agricultural work in a Yorkshire market town." The principal, D V Sinclair, paid him £4 a week.

Alf, city-bred in Scotland, almost needed an interpreter when encountering country folk in Yorkshire to whom dialect was standard speech. In Wensleydale, he would hear about John Thwaite, dialect writer. Perhaps someone quoted a few lines penned after he was attacked by midges:

> *When t'midges land than t'neck yan wipes*
> *An' [hay]reeaks er dropped an' fooak leet pipes.*
>
> *Hoo [how] t'lile beggars make yan scrat,*
> *Midges allis see te that!*
>
> *Neea shakkin' off, neea good te pleean,*
> *They help therselfs te fat an' lean.*
>
> *T'owdest worker – sixty, mooar,*
> *Nivver knew 'em wass [worse] afoor.*

J Fairfax-Blakeborough, a frequent contributor to *The Dalesman*, unearthed (or unstabled) a number of horsy words that had become an accepted part of everyday speech – *muck-sweeat, stalled, gannin' crammelly* (moving badly) and *fadge* (to go at the slowest pace).

Gwen Wade, another contributor, recalled what was said when a woman with a stomach disorder visited the doctor: "'At's bin natterin' me summat chronic. Eh! An' I were dowly! I'd t'ditherum-dotherums all o' t'dea…" A telling expression of a burying was: "We've getten him put sideways."

My interview with Alf occasionally lapsed into dialect, at which both of us smiled. His writing career had began, with encouragement from his wife Joan. Unable to use his real name for professional reasons, he needed a pseudonym. Football being one of Alf's passions, he was watching a televised match and admired the skill and acrobatics of Jim Herriot, a Scot who was keeping goal for Birmingham.

The name Jim Herriot did not appear in an official list of vets. Alf adopted it for his principal character. (Years later, the original Jim Herriot, footballer, visited Alf at Thirsk. They joyfully kicked and headed a football in the long garden extending behind the surgery).

I commented – Yorkshirewise – that Alf's face was "a good colour". He told me he had been out and about, in the garden or on the hills, during most of a long sunny spell. At the mention of "colour", Alf laughed and recalled his young days as a vet visiting the dalehead farms with their memorable residents. "When they said you'd a bad colour, you got worried. I'm not a very ruddy individual really but was told: 'Thou's lost a bit o' ground since I saw you last, Mr Wight.' Or: 'I think you've failed a bit, you know'."

As a newly qualified vet, Alf had entered the farming world with a special knowledge of five species of animal – horse, ox, sheep, pig and dog. "The dog was the last one and the poor old cat never got a mention...The world of the vet was 'large animal' orientated. We were trained as horse-doctors right through." Everything else was secondary.

"It was rather absurd, for although there were a fair number of horses around when I qualified, you could see that the tractor had taken over almost completely. You didn't see many horse-drawn carts in the street..."

Yorkshire had been renowned for its horses, the horse-dealers being well-known for their shady practices, not least theft. George Borrow wrote that if you shake a halter over a Yorkshireman's grave, he'll rise

Alf and Jim Herriot, the goalkeeper after whom the fictional vet was named, adapt the game of football in the garden behind the Thirsk surgery. (Jim Wight collection)

up and steal it. At Yarm Fair, a man bought a horse from a gipsy and on the way home discovered he was half-a-crown short in his change. He returned to Yarm, confronting the gipsy, who said: "I'll not give you half-a-crown. Tak another nag instead."

Alf, ensconced at Thirsk, found himself in "a quiet little place." Donald Sinclair, whose practise it was, had business links with Frank Bingham, a vet based on Leyburn, in Wensleydale. "The trouble with Frank was that it was just at the beginning of the tuberculin-testing scheme. He couldn't do it, being a man of 58. I was just 24. So they called on us at Thirsk to provide another man." That man was Alf. There now began a love affair with the Pennine dale-country.

Frank Bingham, a tall, fair-haired, blue-eyed Irishman, had a Swiss wife called Emmy and two sons, living at a small house called *Tyrella*. Mrs Bingham, a talented lady, served up some wonderful meals. Alf, having set off from Thirsk to Leyburn with a pack of cheese sandwiches to nourish him during the day, found to his delight that Emmy fed him on stews, apple pies and cakes.

Alf visited Leyburn on three days a week, setting off from Thirsk at about 6 a.m and returning the same evening after a busy day. Leyburn impressed Alf by dint of its enormous market place. "When I first knew the place, it had its grocer's shop, a fishmonger's and a butcher's. And that was about it. It was a one-horse town if ever I saw one." Many apocryphal tales were told about Frank. "He was a wonderful chap. One of my favourite men. He was very kind to me. Frank had a car, though some vets were still going about on motor-bikes."

A magic moment in his early association with the Yorkshire Dales came after he had been motoring over Bellerby Moor, from Leyburn to Grinton. He drew the car off the unfenced road to let out the dog. Sitting on a rock outcrop, he looked along the valley of the Swale towards Richmond. He was struck by the beauty of the area. "I felt as though I had suddenly been transported into a magical land."

Working horses were still around when Alf qualified – "we were trained as horse doctors right through." (R T Walker)

Model of a typical cart to be found at most Dales farms during this period.

Mass gathering of sheep – the animal that was third on the list of species requiring special knowledge for a newly qualified vet.

Our amiable chat over, I took a few photographs, thanked Alf profusely and drove back down the village. At the first opportunity, I stopped to check the tape-recorder. A passing villager looked surprised when he heard Alf's voice emanating from a metal box.

Alf's first spell of work almost entirely centred round cattle. Here a stethoscope is used to check the condition of one of Arthur Dand's cows. (Life magazine)

2

AMONG THE DALESFOLK

Alf's first spell of work in the Dales was concerned almost entirely with tuberculin-testing cattle. As related, Frank Bingham, the vet at Leyburn offered the lucrative tuberculin-testing job to Donald Sinclair. He passed on the practical aspects to Alf, who recalled: "A week's work in Thirsk would bring in from £3 to £5. A week's TB testing earned between £20 and £30. You could see where the work was."

The Dales formed an eradication area in which testing was compulsory. TB was a threat to humans as well as cattle, leading to the death of some of those who drank milk from infected stock. In the old days, when there were no plastic gloves, vets suffered from brucellosis and consequent undulant fever, a depressive illness.

Alf met farmers who were dabbling with "cures" not far removed from Black Magic. That was probably what motivated him to write a book in the first place. "It was a very funny time in veterinary practice, with all those awful old treatments."

Irene Megginson, a contributor to *The Dalesman*, wrote about the "Vitnarry" shelf at a typical farm, on which - travelling in winter presenting many difficulties for vets who lived several miles away - a farmer kept various remedies, often home-made. The old "fellon drinks" administered with the help of a "three gill" bottle were to be succeeded by injections.

The most widespread breed of cattle was the Shorthorn. Alf described it as a "pretty, gentle animal", adding that it was subject to "all those awful old treatments". A cow went down. The farmer would say it had "a worm in its tail." The cow couldn't get up. So they cut off its tail. Another farmer kept a billy goat (which stank) in the shippon to prevent

Alf with herdsman Sam Goldsbrough treating cow for infertility. (Jim Wight collection)

Alf chats with a farmer without interrupting his busy routine. (Jim Wight collection)

contagious abortion. "He thought the smell would help to cure the complaint." Abortion hit a herd only once. The animals developed an immunity. The billy goat got the credit.

Jim Wight recalled for me when the vet was a member of a macho-profession. "You stripped to the waist, summer and winter, for almost every task." The vet spent an inordinate amount of time with his arms up bovine orifices. As Siegfried used to say: "There's a whole lot to be learned up a cow's backside." (Scanners are now being used. The old pregnancy diagnosis no longer applies).

During Alf's daily motor ride to Leyburn, and his round of farms, he left a temperate zone for the wild, bleak scenery of the upper dales. It made a strong appeal, as Jim Wight recalls: "Get him up on to Tan Hill and he would stand and take deep breaths. Then he'd say: 'My, but this air's fantastic'."

He was doubtless told the story of the Swaledale farmer who had a horse and cart that was regularly drawn up outside Tan Hill inn. The farmer bought a whisky – for his horse. He wouldn't buy one for himself, explaining: "It wouldn't be right. I'm driving."

A moor that appeared to be a monotonous tract of heather was, indeed, a tight mosaic of stunted plants, tolerating extreme conditions – high rainfall and searching wind. Ling, bell heather, bilberry, cotton grass, sphagnum moss throve in this sodden, elevated situation.

The type of hill farm Alf visited formed part of a "fellside culture", in which a farmer stoically coped with thin soils, a high rainfall and protracted winters. Haytime was as late as July. Grass, mown by scythe, wilted in sunlight and breeze before being transported along a steep hillside by horse-drawn sled.

Alf met a kind-hearted people. "They say that a spectator sees most of the game and I – as a young Glaswegian – was looking at them purely from the outside. I remember chatting to a man aged about sixty. Just over the fell-top, some five miles away, as the crow flies, was some marvellous countryside. He had never been there. He lived in his own little dale and went into Leyburn on market day. That was it…"

It was a time when cows were hand-milked, often in their summer grazings, the three-legged stool being left on a wall-top when not in use. When indoor milking became common, a crusty old farmer remarked: "Milk tastes o' nowt 'til a cow's had its foot in t'bucket." Milk was transported to the farmhouse by back-can or in cans strapped to donkeys; here it was hand-churned till it "broke" as butter, which a hard-working farmer's wife then took to market in a basket, hoping for a quick sale.

Lower down the dale, where herds were larger, milk was transported to the railway station or dairy in tapered kits, which had plenty of weight at their base. They were devised for rolling at an angle, controlled by movements of the hands. A railway porter who regularly received such kits from farmers who delivered them by horse and cart, might roll a kit as fast as he could walk.

Alf's written tales were of real people with individual outlook and behaviour. He admired their fortitude. He latched on to their pithy humour. Farmers and their families spent most of their time in sparse and draughty stone-flagged kitchens. Many farmers, not being able to afford a car, cycled to market, overtaking the walking postman.

The dales that lay between tracts of moorland teemed with rich characters. Alf observed: "The higher up the dale you went, the more unique and nicer was the type of person you met… I was lucky. Farms were so isolated the people loved to see somebody from the outside world.

"The families were generally large. After I had done the tuberculin 'test' they would say: 'Come in and have a bit o' dinner.' This was the great saying; they were so hospitable. Before the agricultural reps were going around, and there were regular visitors, everyone would 'down tools'

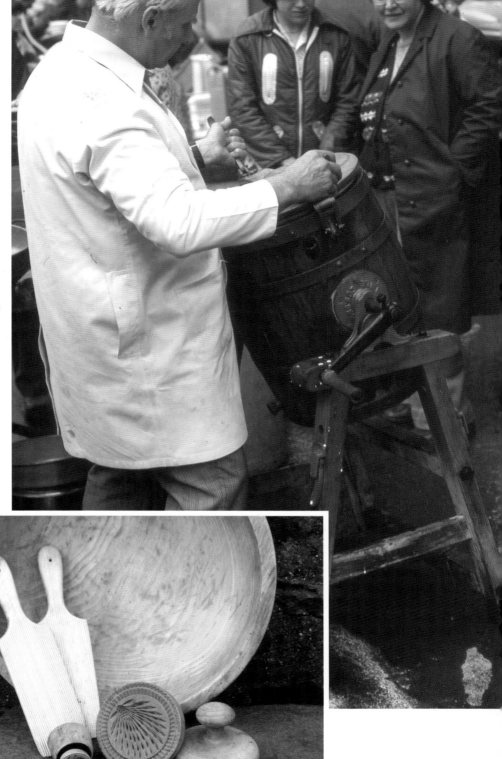

Opposite: Examining a calf with Brian Fountain of Boltby during the period when cattle were occupying much of Alf Wight's time. (Yorkshire Post Newspapers)

Butter-making was still part of traditional farm life when Alf started work in the Dales. These photos show a typical butter churn and a selection of the utensils that were used.

and sit round and look at me."

When I chatted with Alf, he recalled his updale visitors and a typical kitchen of a dalehead farmstead. The kitchen was "a big flagged place. Enormous. You couldn't help but feel sorry for the women who had to work in such a cold, draughty place. The farmer's wife who opened the door very often had an apron made of sacking. Sometimes she had clogs on her feet."

Entering the kitchen, Alf would see a low, brown, earthenware sink, which was almost literally back-breaking to use. Huge sides of fat bacon hung from hooks driven into the ceiling. "You had to duck your head to avoid brushing against them. Bacon was what they lived on. Every time you went into a kitchen there was this lovely smell of bacon being cooked. But it was nearly all fat. And I can't eat fat."

In the living kitchen, the fireplace was part of a wrought-iron range incorporating oven and wash-boiler. "There'd be a reckan they pulled out and hung the kettle on. They made some wonderful Yorkshire puddings. I remember that."

Before the coming of electricity, a fire to provide hot water was maintained the year through, even on the most blistering day. A big iron kettle always had a song in its heart and the boiler was kept well filled with water that could be drawn off by tap. Once a week, the kitchen range was given an application of black-lead that restored the gleam to its face.

Anyone who was fastidious with regard to food was known as *kysty*. In days when nearly everybody felt peckish, they ate all that was put before them. A farm man who tripped up in a distant pasture when the dinner bell was sounded said to another: "There's no point in rushing. Bi t'time we get there, all t'food 'll hev been 'etten."

Moorland peat, cut and stacked to dry, then moved to the farms by horse and sled, provided the bulk of winter fuel at many a farm. A load was painstakingly transported to the farm by horse and two-wheeled cart.

Alf soon realised that families on the uplands were thrifty but helped one another. A farm lass who had a three mile walk from home to schoolhouse one morning saw a group of sad people at a farm – one of the smallest farms, having only two acres of meadow. The only horse they owned had dropped dead. Her father gave her sixpence and said: "Get me the cheapest notebook they sell at the village shop...and don't spend anything on sweets."

Years later, while going through her dead father's possessions, she came across the little notebook. In it was a list of farmers her father had contacted – and what they gave to the luckless family towards the cost of a new horse.

Alf was amazed at the hardiness of the dalesmen. "I was in my twenties. I'd see a fellow in his 70s shovelling away in the teeth of a cutting wind. 'It's blowing a bit thin this morning,' he would say. He'd just have a jacket on and I'd a muffler and a heavy overcoat. They were hardy fellows."

At snowtime, he might do the first injections of the cattle at an upland farm – and then find that, because of a blizzard, he could not get back to do the second injection. "I had to start all over again." It was a period of grim winters. The denizens of Compstone Hill Farm, just over the hill from Cotterdale, saw snow begin to fall one Thursday.

The blizzard did not blow itself out until Sunday. Groceries and loads of coal were conveyed up the fields by horse and coup – a form of sled with a box on it, used mainly for carrying muck to the pastures. Such a sled might hold 5 cwt of coal.

The time Alf spent with Frank Bingham was enjoyable, though in common with a lot of vets at the time, Frank was virtually an alcoholic. Jim told me: "Get him into the *Wensleydale Heifer* at West Witton, the *CB* in Arkengarthdale, or one of several pubs in Leyburn, and you

Curios from the days of the wrought-iron range are displayed alongside a modern fireplace.

Mounted shepherd 'kenning' sheep on the high moors above Swaledale.

couldn't get him out." He was nonetheless one of Alf's all-time favourite human beings; he would appear in the plot of his third book, *Let Sleeping Dogs Lie*, under the name Ewan Ross.

Frank, a charming, laid-back man who didn't care, was not well known to American readers of the Herriot books. Unaccountably, Ewan Ross was severely edited in their editions. Frank had special skills, being the only man known to Alf who might cast a wild colt with one hand while rolling a cigarette with the other!

Casting a colt was one thing; attending to a horse was quite another. Alf was familiar with the ordinary working horse. John Oswald Dinsdale, the Hawes blacksmith, described his work with horses as "blood for money". He had been knocked about by the stags [unbroken ponies, fresh from the fells] which were sold at the autumn horse fair. When breaking-in a lively pony, some dalesmen filled an old pair of trousers with straw and strapped them to the back of the animal, which thus became accustomed to carrying a man.

A horse with a bit of a cough lost condition and was said to be "brokken-winded". Alf would look at the movement of its ribs as it breathed. "If you got what they called the 'double lift' you knew straight away it was hopeless. It was a thing mainly of draught horses. I'm not sorry to see the draught horse disappear because of the way they used to plod away. The willing horse. That's a good phrase."

A sturdy type of pony – a miniature cart horse, indeed – was also known as a Dales cob. For as long as anyone could remember – and for many years before that – the farmers of the northern dales had benefited from this breed, which was able to perform quite heavy jobs, such as drawing carts of coal from the pits on Tan Hill. A cartload, some 8 cwt of coal, represented the contents of two mine tubs.

The Dales pony was a grand little shaft horse, with strength and stamina. It was also economical, thriving on waste ground where other breeds would starve. A Jack-of-all-trades on many dale-country farms, the breed was becoming uncommon in Alf's day. Tractor and pick-up truck ousted them from the fields and roads. The whiff of petrol fumes became detectable on the uplands.

Frank Bingham was a good vet. What he objected to was the paperwork connected with tuberculin-testing. And once Alf came to grips with this aspect, Frank would say: "Oh, while you're at such-and-such a farm, just castrate a couple of colts."

Bit by bit, Alf became a tester and a practitioner. "I got to know every nook and cranny. Right up to Gayle in Wensleydale and beyond Keld in Swaledale and away up to the head of Coverdale. It was through Frank Bingham that I learned all about my dales...I was young and tireless."

In my own young, tireful days at *The Dalesman*, I was invited to afternoon tea at high-lying Bordley, beyond Wharfedale. When the meal was over, the farmer slurred his chair on the flagged floor of the kitchen and rose to announce that he was "bahn to milk". I followed him, across the cobbled yard into an outbarn with tying-up for half a dozen cows. In fact, only one – a "house cow" – remained.

The farmer reached for the traditional three-legged stool and as he coaxed milk from the cow it was like watching a scene from a Herriot film. He had trapped the cow's tail between his old peaked cap and a flank of the animal. This avoided the problem of muck-buttons – lumps of hardened dung caught up in the hairs of the tail. If such a piece struck the face of the milker, a nasty cut might occur.

Alf Wight relied largely on events recorded in his daily diary for his tale-telling. For much of the time, I used a tape-recorder. It picked up authentic voices, such as the daleswoman talking about porridge, a staple food at farm and cottage. "We just about lived on oatmeal porridge and plenty of black treacle, which was a penny a jar. We'd get a bucketful of blue [skimmed] milk for a penny and use it on the porridge."

In another dalehead home, I heard that "we had a big pan, with a handle,

The horse was already becoming uncommon on Dales farms in Alf's day, but was long a key part of haytime.

Kisdon Gorge, upper Swaledale.

and we put it on the reckan, over an open fire. We'd pour into the pan some skimmed milk. When it was nearly on the boil, we'd scatter oatmeal in. If you put the meal in too fast, you had lumps called *dog 'eeards.* If you had a fall of soot, you had sooty porridge."

When my tape-recorder was a novelty – both to me and the subject of the interview – I visited a farm high above Garsdale and said to the farmer: "Do you mind if I tape this conversation?" Not sure of what I meant, he did not object. During the interview, he got het-up about the new conifer plantations.

We chatted – and were recorded – for the best part of an hour. Then I wound back at random the tape in my recorder so he could hear part of the conversation. It so happened that when I switched on the topic was – new conifer plantations. The dalesman rose to his feet and said in a loud voice: "I telled thee I was reight. Yon chap agrees wi' me."

I took the recorder to Tan Hill, one of Alf's favourite haunts, when the annual show of Swardles [Swaledale sheep] took place. A vacant moor, adjacent to the highest licensed premises in the land, filled up with humanity and some of the best sheep in the Dales. I saw families with names that are truly of the Dales – Alderson (a surname selected by Alf for Helen) and Raine, Harker and Calvert, Garnett and Blades.

Alf was familiar with cattle being over-wintered in little outbarns. The slopes of the dales were speckled with hundreds of outbarns, situated where there was a natural run-off of water. Cattle were released from winter bondage daily to drink.

In upper Swaledale, an outbarn was a *field house.* Or *cowhouse.* To the farmer of the northern dales it might be known as a *coo-us.* Cattle were tied up in an outbarn from November until May, being released briefly during the day to go to water, the source of which was either a small watercourse trickling down the fellside or a spring.

Within an outbarn, a small number of cattle were accommodated in a shippon or *liggin*. Doors provided access to the shippon and *mewstead*, the last-named being the storage point for hay made in adjacent meadows. Alf was enchanted by the local terms. Each barn had a *forking hole*, high up, to which hay was transferred from a laden cart. Above the shippon were the *baulks*, bare boards providing storage for yet more hay.

Into the barn went hay. Out of the barn, more precisely the shippon, and into a special midden, went the dung, commonly known as *muck*, plus old bedding such as bracken. A horse and sled might be used to distribute this across the land in small heaps, from which it would be spread finely by hand-fork, thus nourishing the next crop of grass.

Outbarns provided unofficial lodgings for the many tramps who wandered through the dale-country. Sleeping in a barn was a chancy business. One tramp ran the risk of decapitation when a farmer, not knowing he was there, used a *mew spade* to cut hay before feeding it to the stock. The farmer stopped work when a tramp raised his arm above the stack of hay.

Alf originally toured the Dales farmers using "a funny old Austin 10". All vets were impecunious in every way. "This car had no heater, of course. The floor was shattered and every time I went over a puddle the muddy water would splash up into my face. The windscreen had become so cracked that there was only one or two places I could peer through. Amazingly, it took me on my rounds, up hill and down dale."

There was one terrible period when the brakes did not work. "We couldn't get around to sorting them out, so I drove all over those hilly places without being able to use them. I put a bit in my book about travelling into West Witton from the moortop and negotiating that terrible hairpin bend without any brakes on the car. I wouldn't do that now if you gave me a million pounds."

Curiously, as an emissary of *The Dalesman*, I had the Herriot-like transition to ownership of a car – a 1939 Ford, which had been modified

Features of Gunnerside in upper Swaledale:
Top left: Hooping stone at the smithy (the blacksmith received a wheel from the joiner and attached a metal rim).
Top right: Inn sign at the Kings Head.
Bottom: Gunnerside Gill, showing some of the ruined buildings associated with lead mining.

Austin van of 1934 vintage at a Pickering rally. It is the type of vehicle used by young vets at the time.

to the extent that part of the flooring was composite board and resting on it was a chair larger and heavier than that originally intended. My garage man, asked to pass judgement on the car when it was noisier than usual, said: "It's got tappet-rattle, piston slap – and a crack in the chassis."

Like Alf, I motored in a tract of wild country. Unlike Alf I experienced a sinking feeling. There had been a wet spell, the composite boarding was sagging and breaking away, giving me an unusual downward view of the passing stretch of road. I managed to reach a village with a joiner, who effected repairs. Wooden floorboards were fitted – and creosoted!

I met some rare old characters. Alf would have delighted to be in the company of George Metcalfe, of Appersett, whom I found sitting by the bridge, clay pipe in mouth, old cap high on the back of his head and well down over his eyes, high cheeks bristling with grey hairs that eventually merged with a bushy moustache.

He told me that he had never seen the sea. A pause. "It's nobbut watter." Another pause, then: "I don't suppose many people have seen Appersett." Our conversation switched to drystone walls. An American called them "those cute stone fences." George was an experienced waller. He had charged 3s a rood – in Yorkshire, seven yards - for his work.

Annie Mason, of Hawes, told me that on a visit to Manchester her mother had bought a novelty called a thermos flask. She made use of it at a time when sheep that had been wintered in Wharfedale were being driven back over Fleet Moss to the home farms in Wensleydale. One of the drovers, thankful for the offer of coffee, was handed the thermos, the cap having been removed. He drank deeply – and yelled as the liquid, unexpectedly hot, coursed down his throat!

The Yorkshire Dales was predominantly sheep-country. Dalesmen were obsessed with sheep, their tough breed taking its name, Swardle, from Swaledale. The type was set by farmers living on and around Tan Hill. Small-time farmers thought a lot about their sheep. Curiously, a sheep never seemed to be ill for long. It either recovered or died.

Jim Wight had seen the opposite situation apply, when an "owd yow" that had been torn to bits during lambing procedures miraculously lived. "One of Dad's favourite tales was attending a sheep at Angram Grange that was sunken-eyed, having suffered so badly during lambing that Dad said to the farmer: 'Look, I'm not going to charge you but I'll give her a large dose of barbituate and put her out of her pain; she's going to die'."

A week later, Alf was called to another lambing yow at the same farm. The farmer pointed to a grazing sheep and said: "That's the one you gave the injections to." Dad said: "I thought I'd given her a shot to kill her." The farmer replied: "Nay – she slept for three days then she got up and she wanted a bit of hay. The dose she had received had put the sheep out of her pain and she'd had those three days of sleep and rest before starting eating again. Sheep are amazing creatures."

An old-time topic that fascinated me was sheep-salving. A farmer made a mixture of butter and Stockholm tar "wi' a drop o' milk to tak the sting out of it." A sheep's wool was methodically parted, exposing strips of skin, to which the salve was applied. Salved sheep were supposed to winter better than untouched animals. Salved made the hands black. One of the family was married at salving time. His hands were jet black for the ceremony.

At a show, I asked a farmer about the condition of the sheep after a grim winter. "Nay – thou won't be able to tell at this show," said he. "This lot will have bin in t'parlour. It's them sheep out theer" – and he pointed across the misty moor – "that's t'yardstick!"

Another batch of sheep arrived. The animals stood exhaling grey vapour into the grey mist. A farmer wi' nowt much to do shouted to the new arrival: "Dusta want 'em up here?" There was a nod. The farmer turned to the intervening group of visitors and requested them to stand clear with the words: "Just make a 'ole."

**Hawes, 'capital' of
upper Wensleydale.**

Sheepdogs in Swaledale.

Opposite: Alf with newborn lamb, about 1975. (Derek Bayes)

Sheep shearing in the days well before electric clippers. Left: A sheep being clipped on a creel at Kettlewell – an operation with which Alf would be totally familiar.

Moss-crop, an early stage in the formation of "cotton grass", was a useful early bite for sheep. One of the old-time farmers said a sheep could see it before he could. "You could tell when they were mossin' because they grovelled about in it with their noses which became bright wi' rubbing." Too much of the stuff led to a "moss" illness called "staggers". Dales farmers lost a lot o' sheep to staggers. They couldn't do much about it until clever folk produced medicines.

Bill Alderson claimed that sheep benefit from being on mixed ground - "first on the heather and then on the 'white ground'. Heather-land was good at t'back-end of t'year. It doesn't muck up, doesn't heather. You can have more sheep to the acre on heather than green ground because it doesn't get *foiled* [affected by sheep droppings] the same."

Bill recalled "t'owd days" when dozens of sheep, overblown by snow, inhabited small snow-caves. "If they get under a hagg where there's a bit o' room, they can nebble and nebble away...I've heard my dad say two sheep that were found had been liggin' under snow for days. One sheep had etten t'wool off t'other. They'd eat peat if there was nowt else."

How did a farmer find snowbound sheep? "I've fun 'em all sorts o' ways – sometimes deeard!" Snowdrifts were prodded with rake shafts. This indicated where sheep were lying. Or a sheep's breath might open up an air passage from which scent could spread, attracting a collie dog with a good nose. "A dog that's used to it walks on t'wind side so it gets t'scent."

Bill told me of a day in March when "it came on sharp. There was no snaw to be seen t'night afore. It came on through t'night." Thirty sheep were overblown. Looking for them, Bill left his horse where the snow was getting deep and walked the last few miles. He then "dug out and dug out...Dogs were getting done and I was getting done."

He set off back home, calling at a farm on the way. T'chap gave me a cup o' tea. And by gow – but I was pleased. I'd had nowt to drink and my food had got mashed up in my pocket as I shovelled snow. Day mended. I'd left t'horse further down. I was glad when I got to her. It was maybe half past ten when I got back home. It 'd bin an hard day..."

In my *Dalesman* travels, I heard of doctoring carried out at home, using old remedies. Warts could be dealt with by burying meat – a piece of meat for each wart – in the garden. One dalesman was reputed to "charm" warts away. His skill was put to the test by a dalesman who had an unsightly wart that was exposed to the dalesman's charm. When a friend inquired about the wart, he was told the charmer had been useless; he still had the wart. He felt for it. It had gone!

Alf, a weekday visitor to the dale-country during his early vethood, never became aware of the depth of religious feeling among the dalesfolk. Especially for Methodism. Each parish had an Anglican church. Alf and his family attended the mini-cathedral of St Mary at Thirsk. Yet most families were "chapil folk".

There seemed to be a chapel every few miles, some being solitary buildings attended by farmfolk who, dressed in "Sunday best", invariably walked to worship. On the Lord's Day, the normal sounds were hushed. The word *thou* for "you", frequently used, surely emanated from the Authorised version of the Bible which many dalesfolk heard weekly and read in their evening prayers. Variations on the word were *thoo*, *tha* and *thi*. A daleswoman who objected to her husband's prattlings was heard to say: "Doan't thee-thou me!"

As a Methodist local preacher in the Yorkshire Dales for forty years, I recall when chapels were well supported, prayers were fervent and extempore, hymn-singing lusty and a chorus of "amens" acknowledged a well-made point in the sermon. Just before my first solo appearance as a preacher, the duty steward said: "Are you nervous, lad?" I nodded. "Nay," said he, "we should be more freightened of thee than thou is of us!"

At one solitary chapel, the organist played a harmonium – an "ill wind that nobody blows any good" – and on cold days a fire burned brightly in a grate. When the chapel was built, it had taken the form of adjacent

Sheep-salving was once as much a part of the farming year as sheep-washing, when wash dubs such as this one at Stonesdale Commmon, above Swaledale, would resound to almost continuous bleating.

Studied concentration in Wensleydale:

A visitor checks his map beside Coverham Abbey, which is on private land.

Over: Sheep peers through a window at the ruined Old Church near Semerwater.

houses which, if the chapel did not succeed, could revert to housing. At Timble, in the Washburn Valley, where I conducted harvest festival services, candles and oil lamps augmented the feeble daylight. The hymn-singing was accompanied by a lady who strummed the keys of a battery-operated Yamaha.

At Mount Zion, Tosside, a chapel of the Old Independency, eventually open for worship only four times a year, I occupied a pulpit so lofty it was like being on the bridge of a small coaster. In the centre of the chapel glowed a huge coke stove, white-hot in the gloom. The bride at a wedding walked so close to the stove, her veil might get *frizzled*.

I knew a moor-edge chapel so isolated that lapwings nested on tousled land round about. Curlews bubbled over with song as they sail-planed over meadows that would not be disturbed until a July haytime. From the pulpit I looked over a row of babies in carry-cots to the main congregation.

In a back-pew were half a dozen crusty old men, one of whom – during my somewhat fanciful children's address – shouted: "We want none o' thi fairy tales here."

Tales were told of unorthodox preachers who were kept back in the vestry and challenged on points they had raised in their sermons. As the number of little farms – and farm folk – declined, so did the number of chapels. Tales of "chapil days" remained. I heard of a farmer who, in a Dales equivalent of Paul's vision while on the road to Damascus, recalled: "I wor crossing t'top pasture wi' a cow bucket when I saw a breet light in t'sky. (A pause). I were that capped, I nearly dropped t'bucket."

Total abstinence was preached and practised. A small boy, asked by a Sunday School teacher if he could write his name, shook his head. "When you can, tell me," said the teacher. On the great day, the lad was invited to show the teacher how he wrote his name. She provided the paper. He obliged – and years later discovered that he had signed the

Dales farmer with twin lambs.

**Farmer with sheep near
Aysgarth, Wensleydale.**

Pledge to refrain from strong drink.

Baptists and Congregationalists staked their claim in the religious life of the locality before Methodism established itself in a region of lonely fells and dales thinly scattered with farms and villages. The buildings had a sameness in design, the body of the chapel being almost box-like, with a steep roof and a tiny porch stuck on as though it were an afterthought. Some of the grandest chapels are in the old lead-mining area of Swaledale.

An early mode of transport to out-of-the-way chapels was a push-bike. A fellow preacher, cycling to an appointment at a fellside chapel against a head wind, prayed to the Lord that the wind would change direction. It did. He had a head wind on the return home.

Alf bemoaned the passing of the old type of Yorkshire farmer – t'old chap who had half a dozen cows, treated them with black magic remedies and spoke the Yorkshire dialect. Not all the characters in his books have our sympathy. Yet in Herriot's world, justice and basic human kindness usually triumphed in the end.

Big changes were in prospect. The farm horse would be supplanted by the "lile grey Fergie", as a popular Ferguson model was known. It was relatively cheap, low-geared and adroit – having affinities with a horse, in fact - ideally suited to a dalehead farm. I recalled that the foot-brake was apt to slip a little when dew formed on a haytime evening. Then an untended tractor and laden haycart would trundle slowly towards a drystone wall, being usually spotted and stopped in good time.

Ancient bottled remedies were items for the history book when antibiotics and other treatments arrived. In the 1930s, once-isolated farmsteads were being linked by good roads, along which petrol-driven vehicles passed at the rate of about two an hour. The dalesfolk now had high mobility and ready access to urban facilities. Meanwhile, the old-time vet spent most of his time on farms, attending to cattle and sheep, up to his arm in the rump of a cow having difficulty with calf birth or

Farm transactions: Hand-clasp to seal a bargain, photographed at an auction mart in lower dale country.

A Dales farm sale.

Ornamental head of a shepherd's crook, carved by one of the Fawcett family.

Hannah Hauxwell, best known of the womenfolk who have played a major part in Dales life.

taking the temperature of a sheep when disease was suspected.

In this book, I am not competing with Alf, the master storyteller. In his later days, Alf was inclined adroitly to transfer tales he heard in the 1950s and 60s back to the 1930s and 40s. I write from my own experiences of folk in the James Herriot age and from conversations with the Wight family, father and son. An authentic insight into old-time Dales life came when I joined *The Dalesman* magazine in 1948, editing it until my retirement forty years later.

I was married for 55 years to Freda, a farmer's daughter whose family had connections with the upper valley of the Wharfe. My first visit to the farm on the Gledstone estate where Freda lived, was in the 50s – and coincided with haytime. Invited to go on the *moo*, a lyrical term I found appealing, I scrambled on to an oven-hot and dusty *mewstead*, forking new hay under beams draped with king-sized cobwebs.

A man who told me of the first mowing machine seen in the area mentioned it was drawn by two horses. "Ay! I don't know," he remarked. "T'herbs'll nivver grow when they've run a machine on 'em."

At the farm where Freda was raised, and from which she cycled to work, I saw evidence of her father's prowess at culling "pests". On my first visit, as a town-lad, I winced at the sight of a section of fence adorned by the bodies of slain crows. In January, Dad listened for the gruff voices of lovelorn dog foxes – and neatly despatched many of them.

One mealtime, hearing the cackling of hens, he rose from the dinner table, grabbed a shotgun, dashed outdoors and up a ladder he had shrewdly reared against a high wall. Bang! He had shot a stoat that was threatening his poultry!

Alf Wight would have been amused another time when Dad settled at the fireside, easing himself on to a cane chair (with a black fleece draping the back). He put his head in his hands and gave such a sigh it could have won a drama award in another setting. Said Freda's long-suffering mother: "I wish I had Dad's cold."

Womenfolk have played a major part in Dales life. The aforementioned Annie Mason, a young lady who lived at the head of Wensleydale, scrambled out of bed in the early hours so she might drive her father, James Pratt, auctioneer and cattle dealer, to Garsdale station for a train that left for Scotland at 6 a.m. On cold, dark mornings, the dutiful daughter put two heavy coats over her night-dress so that father would not be delayed.

When she returned home, passing through Appersett, dear old Mrs Buck would be waiting for her with a cup of hot cocoa, remarking: "You know, love, I'm sure you'll be starved." She remembered a ride from Ingleton, over Newby Head, on a foggy day. A phenomenon called Willie wi' t'wisp appeared. The horse's mane appeared to shine.

She joined the annual drive of sheep from Wether Fell to wintering quarters at Brimham Rocks, in Nidderdale. "I rode a mare out, then tied the bridle up so that it would not drag, turned the horse round, slapped her on her buttocks – and she returned home of her own accord."

A lovely grey mare belonging to her family had a foal and they were taken to Middleham Moor to be sold. Not being disposed of on the first day, mare and foal were left there until the second. That night, the young lady cried, fearing that she would not see them again. "During the night I heard our grey mare come up the paddock at the back of the house. I jumped out of bed and put the window down and shouted out: 'Our old gal's come back!'"

Yorkshire humour is realistic. A farmer sold a horse. It was returned, with the words: "Yon hoss is no good; it wean't 'od its head up." Said the farmer: "It's pride, lad. Thee get it paid for."

Big changes come to the
Dale country as the tractor
replaces the horse.

Countersett, Wensleydale. (Janet Rawlins)

LIFE AT SKELDALE HOUSE

The Skeldale House described in the Herriot books was 23 Kirkgate, Thirsk, an imposing Georgian house with white-painted doorway and window frames. Jim, in his autobiography of "the real James Herriot", noted that Alf arrived to take up his veterinary duties here on 18th July, 1940.

Allocated one of the upstairs rooms, he and Joan decked it with second-hand furniture, much of it bought at sales. They treated themselves to an oak coffee table on which had been carved the figure of a mouse, devised and carved at the workplace of Robert Thompson, of Kilburn. Alf expended a few last shillings on the purchase.

Railings fronted Kirkgate. Ivy climbed untidily over mellow brick to the topmost windows. A long, relatively narrow walled garden was a prime feature in summer when it was in marked contrast with the big, shabby rooms of the house. In his book *If Only They Could Talk*, Alf recalled his first glimpse of the garden – unkempt lawns, a rockery and many fruit trees.

"A great bank of peonies blazed in the hot sunshine and at the far end, rooks called in the branches of a group of tall elms...Sunshine beat back from the high old walls, bees droned among the bright masses of flowers. A gentle breeze stirred the weathered blooms of a magnificent wisteria which almost covered the back of the house. There was peace here."

For a few days, Alf travelled round the practice with Donald and Eric Parker to acquaint himself with the area. He signed his contract as a salaried partner on 24 July, and began work two days later.

The Herriot Centre in Kirkgate, Thirsk. The adjoining building is where Alf took up his veterinary duties in July 1940.

Seniority was indicated by professional plates beside the door. Donald had a big brass plate. A smaller, cheaper plate was displayed for Alf. When Jim, Alf's son, mentioned the discrepancy in size and quality of the plates to his father, the reply was unemotional. What mattered most to Alf when he sought a job in 1939 was not so much prestige but Donald Sinclair's gift of a free partnership. Many vets, not being able to get jobs with animals, took whatever work they could find. "Dad said he would not have worried if his 'plate' had been made of a bit of plywood or even of paper. He had a partnership. 'I'd got my nose in the trough'."

Donald Sinclair, senior partner in the veterinary practice. (Jim Wight collection)

A chance remark in 1996 put me on the trail of Donald V. Sinclair, who became widely known through the Herriot books and films as Siegfried Farnon. I picked up Donald's trail in Settle, North Ribblesdale, where in 1937 and 1938 he served as an adviser to the Ministry of Agriculture. A dear not-so-young lady I met at a McEvoy family reunion had clear memories of Donald. His name cropped up in our conversation after someone mentioned the recent publication of his will. Donald, who died in 1995, left a tidy sum – £1,133,000.

A busy vet's life in January 1975. (Top) In the office.
(Bottom) Checking equipment in the boot of the car before setting out on farm visits. (Yorkshire Post Newspapers)

In the pre-war days when he toured a district affected by sheep scab, Donald lodged at a semi-detached house in Duke Street, Settle. He dated a local girl. My informant – her sister, then aged eight – was asked by her mother to act as chaperone.

The Donald of popular recollection was a dashing figure - tall, thin, sandy-haired, neatly-moustached, not unlike Errol Flynn, a film hero of the time. Young ladies in the North Craven area were inclined to swoon as he drove past them in his blue Lagonda.

Donald left the Ministry and, moving to Thirsk, having bought a practice from an elderly Mr Wood, developed the veterinary coverage of the area. Donald – and in due course Alf – had a struggle to keep the practice viable. There was little surplus "brass". A farmer with an ailing beast thought twice – sometimes thrice – before calling out a vet.

When Alf fictionalised himself as James Herriot, the Sinclair brothers found prominent places in the storyline – Donald as the aforementioned Siegfried and Brian, a younger brother, as Tristan. Brian became a Ministry man working in Leeds. His friendship with Alf endured and they met each other socially on their half-day visits to Harrogate.

Alf, living just above the poverty line in his early years at Thirsk, had a good memory of out-of-the-ordinary happenings. Instances of Donald's occasional fratchiness, and Brian's great sense of fun, would play key parts in stories he related in print when transformed into highly successful narrative.

Donald, tall, slim, charming, was mercurial – quick to fly off the handle now and again, as I heard when I chatted with Pat McEvoy, whose family lived in the big house at Stackhouse near Settle. Pat got to know Donald Sinclair when he was a pupil Ampleforth College; his regard for him led him to run the eight miles from Ampleforth to Thirsk to dine with Donald and his mother.

It was from Pat that I heard of the Great Hay Fiasco. Donald, arriving

Alf with Bodie, the Border terrier. (Jim Wight collection)

back from the auction mart in a flurry, had just bought a stack of loose hay on a farm some miles beyond Thirsk. Said Pat: "A Scottish cowman called MacMath and I were to go down with him to cut and truss the hay, which would then be loaded on to a tractor-drawn trailer driven by his garage proprietor. Our old horse was obviously not up to it."

Neither of the two men were familiar with this procedure, but they borrowed a hay knife from the farm and set to, realising quite soon that the task required a razor-sharp knife and a lot of very hard work. By the time Donald returned, they had barely a quarter of a load. "Right!" he said, "that will do. Take it back to the farm."

Travelling all that way for so little was a sorry sight. "And at what expense!" The rest of the haystack arrived next day on the back of a wagon. It had been neatly baled. "As it turned out, it was worth its weight in gold." After spending some years on Army service, Pat lived with Donald and his wife Audrey for three months. Audrey was well connected socially and economically. During the summer of 1945 she and Donald had moved from 23 Kirkgate to Southwoods Hall.

Pat's stay at Southwoods coincided with The Great Storm of 1947. In a district clogged with snow, the jeep he had purchased from a Polish flying officer was the most reliable means of taking Donald, the vet, on his rural rounds. Even so, on several occasions the road was solidly blocked by snow and he had to reverse the jeep for considerable distances.

Donald had a big Bentley car, the type with a leather strap across the bonnet. One day, Pat had a puncture while riding his bike from Ampleforth to his home at Stackhouse. The puncture occurred at Kettlewell, in upper Wharfedale. A local man repaired it but, when fitting it back on the wheel, must have nipped it. The tube burst again. Donald, while motoring through the village, assessed Pat's plight and drove him to his family home after arranging for the bike to be taken there by a local carrier.

An unflattering description of Donald would appear in a book, *All Things Herriot*, published in America. The author, Sandford Sternlicht, a professor of Syracuse University, described Farnon as being "hard working, professionally committed, mercurial, short-tempered, forgetful, generous when he is not worried about money, and inconsistent." Donald and Alf worked together for fifty-four years. Pat McEvoy described Donald as a most charming man, for most of the time. He was not recalled as a teller of tales. Said Pat: "It was enough that he was himself."

Jim Wight described Brian Sinclair as "most amusing. If I had to count the best friends of my father on one hand, he would be among them." Brian's main purpose in life was to enjoy himself. He played jokes on people. He told jokes to people. He always carried bits of paper on which he had written jokes.

Jim said: "Whenever my father met him, he always came back with a list of Brian's jokes." Normally quiet, dignified and sound, Brian was inclined to explode into activity after swallowing a couple of drinks. He was fond of doing "party pieces" in pubs.

In the books it is implied that Donald was always shouting and screaming at his brother, which he was, and with good reason. Donald was financing Brian's education and the young brother failed exam after exam. The veterinary colleges did not necessarily want students to pass. "If you took 15 years to pass a five-year-course, that was fine because the college was receiving the fees all the time."

The "nicely appointed" surgery, with its gleaming surfaces, that appeared in the BBC television series *All Creatures Great and Small*, did not exist in the real Skeldale House until the late 1960s or early 1970s. Said Jim: "There was no consulting room. Dogs were brought in and plonked on tables. Vets attended to them wearing tweed jackets and wellies. The waiting room was our living room. Our dining room was the office."

Accountancy was a simple matter of stuffing any money received into a pint pot that reposed on the mantelpiece. "That was the 'book-keeping'." Jim still has the pint pot, which had been issued by Wakefield Cricket Club in 1934. From 1949 onwards, the practice had a secretary who was there to try and sort out the problems of accountability.

Alf and Joan, newly-wed, occupied the top floor of the surgery in Kirkgate. The rooms, unused for years, were musty. They had a bed-sitting room and a kitchen of sorts. There was no running water. Jim was to recall: "All the water had to be brought up three flights of stairs in a stone jug. Dad used to say it was a great start to the day. Two of three trips with the water jug got the circulation moving."

Two gas rings were available and when a square tin was fitted the newly-weds had a makeshift oven. Joan was an acceptable cook. They would occupy those rooms long enough for their small children, Jim and his sister Rosie, to use them as a play area.

In winter, bitter north winds swept the Plain of Mowbray. Jim's over-riding juvenile memory of 23 Kirkgate, Thirsk, was that the place was cold – icy cold in the bedrooms and freezing cold in the bathrooms. "The house had two fires to provide heat for ten rooms. I used to run round this house to keep warm. Dad was keen on fresh air."

During his spell of service in the R.A.F. in the early 1940s, he had been billeted in the *Grand Hotel*, Scarborough, and toughened by exposure to easterly winds blowing unchecked through the dormitories. The windows had been nailed open. Alf carried that fresh-air principle to his family home. Says Jim: "We had the windows open and draughts whistling down the corridors and stone-flagged passages. As a small boy I used to complain. When I said to Dad I felt cold, he would say: 'Well, run about then!' And I did!"

Extending from a long corridor at the back of the house was a kitchen and a scullery. "How did the women of that time manage to wash without washing machines? I remember mother flagging away down

One vet and his dogs:
with Hector, a long-nosed
Jack Russell
... and again with Hector,
a favourite dog, and Dan
(Fay Godwin – 2)

there, then passing the clothes through a wringer before hanging them out on the line."

Alf was unhandy about the house. "We cannot be good at everything in the world. On his own confession he was useless at household tasks." He was non-mechanical. (If his car broke down, he'd no idea how to rectify it).

Jim watched him trying to light a domestic fire in a freezing house. "When it had been lit for half an hour, it was still just a little, black, smoking mound. A white flame would appear for a second or two and then disappear. Mother would have a roaring inferno going within minutes."

From 1945, a family of four – Alf, Joan, Jim and Rosie – became five when they were joined by Laura Danbury, "mum's mother". She was, according to Jim, a charming, quiet, easy-going lady whose presence enabled her daughter to get out of the house more often to do some shopping. "Granny would attend to the telephone. It rang 24 hours a day. She helped my mother greatly."

Mother spent a good deal of her life scrubbing away at stone floors. "That was one reason why we left." Not only did father want a house of his own, but he did not like to see his wife killing herself with housework. Jim was nine years old when the family moved into what in contrast was a tropical paradise. It was a modern house, though without central heating. "My father didn't believe in central heating. At least we had warm rooms and it was draught-free. And we had an Aga in the kitchen. That was the thing! The old kitchen had totally iced up in the winter."

Alf and his family, who had been living at Blakey View in Sowerby, eventually returned to Skeldale House. It was their home for the next eight years.

4

MEN OF SWALEDALE

Tradition is still an important feature of Dales life, as I realised once again when attending the 87th annual show of the Swaledale Open Agricultural and Horticultural Society. This was a thoroughly local event, not some idea dreamed up by a publicity officer. The steward at the gate collected my £1, stamped my hand with the word "Muker" and smiled as a nearby farmer said to me: "Thoo wants to be thankful he didn't clip a bit out of an ear." He asked a latecomer: "Hoo is ta?" The reply was: "All is safely gathered in. Taties oot and cows laid in."

At Muker Show, Alf would have been reassured that Dales life was continuing pretty much as it was. Judging the sheep proceeded along traditional lines. If the judges were over-awed by the presence of some of the keenest flockmasters in the North, they didn't show it. A young judge had already developed the art of dallying so everyone was kept in suspense.

The judges took in the general characteristics of the sheep, then moved closer, parting the wool, testing its quality and looking for "black bits". Ewes suffered a total loss of dignity when they were turned on their backs, then reared into a sitting position, where their bellies sagged. The teats of the animals in this class were carefully examined. They must not have suckled young. "A judge wants to see if tits is reight," said a friendly farmer at my right elbow. "Some tits can be duds."

Alf came to love Swaledale because of broad vistas and a sense of loneliness that appealed to him after a hectic spell of veterinary duty. His eyes ranged over acid moorland that was strong of tone, low in profile, majestic in extent. A walker who visited the moors in late summer, bestrode a succession of purpled ridges and kicked up clouds of white heather pollen at every yard. My old pal Matthew Cherry,

Penned rams at Muker Show.

Judging time at a Dales show.

whose house was tucked away in a fold of the land near Gunnerside, was fond of recalling boyhood days on the Swaledale moors and a truly resident bird – the red grouse. It survived the winter with a plumage that included white-feathered spats.

The red grouse was totally dependent on the heather for food and cover. A cock bird was rufous brown, with bright red wattles that were inflated during courtship and when territory is in dispute. The hen bird, sitting hard on her nest, had lighter-colour. Her young were precocious and seemed capable of flight almost before they were fully feathered.

Matthew told me of boyhood days when he was taught how to "call" grouse. Sitting in a hollow or behind a wall at first light in November, when old birds pair, he would imitate the call of the hen bird and attract the swaggering moorcock. Grandfather had a smoker's wooden pipe with the help of which he could call grouse.

A red grouse is one of few creatures that give life to the Yorkshire moors in winter. A thick plumage affords the bird insulation against the cold and wet. It plucks heather with a short bill and has a gut especially adapted for dealing with such tough and fibrous plant food.

Another personality of the upper dale who knew a lot about grouse was William Alderson, JP. He stood six feet tall and was known to one-and-all as "Gurt Bill up t'Steps". They led to the front door of his farmhouse at Angram.

Bill had heard when grouse were shot over dogs. Sent a little way ahead, the dogs "pointed" at crouching grouse, which could then be flushed. At one time, kites were flown to encourage the grouse to remain still until the dogs drew near. Grouse driving came in with the development of breech-loading guns. It was in early use on the Teesdale moors, a little to the north of Swaledale.

Gurt Bill was not keen on the taste of grouse; it was "aw reight" but "I'se not struck on t'auld uns. My wife's mother was a Wilson, the sister of the gamekeeper. I've heard her say that they used to have to hang some grouse up from August to December and cook 'em when t' Lord of Manor came up for dinner. They hanged yon grouse till they dropped off by t'heeads. That's when they were fit to eat. She was never as fed up as when she was cooking these grouse. They were bad – but some folk still ate 'em!"

To the moors, in spring, came the upland waders. Alf heard golden plover, favouring the ground where vegetation was not too dense; dunlin repairing to peaty areas near tarns; snipe to the rush beds; curlews and lapwings at the moorland fringes. They, the larks and pipits, also the merlin, smallest of our falcons, enlivened with their calls the vast tracts of country that – apart from the croaky grouse calls - had been strangely quiet and still in winter.

From the age of five, Bill Alderson had walked one and a-half miles to school at Keld, using field paths. Eventually, he called at the various outbarns to fodder cattle. (Father did the rounds later, mucking-out and watering the stock). Children took their mid-day meals to school with them. The meals improved at pig-killing time, when they had sausage and "crappins". Tea in tin bottles were arranged near the stove to keep warm.

Bill's home was one of half a dozen with a view of wall-girt meadows and prominently detached Kisdon, a sort of island-hill. Bill's father had started the day off with a bowl of porridge. So did Bill, who remarked: "It's thi belly 'at keeps thi back up!"

He milked his first cow at the age of nine. "I started with a cow that was fairly quiet. I've never milked with a machine." In haytime, aged ten, he mowed grass with a scythe. He watched his mother make butter and cheese. For the separation of the cream for butter, the milk was "set up in bowls" in the cellar. "We used to mark 'em wi' a bit of chalk so we could tell how long they'd stood – for one meal or two meals. The cream was ready when it would hold a penny.

An upper Swaledale haymaker.

Opposite:
Top: A cock black grouse displaying at the lek.
Bottom: Curlew in a Dales meadow.

Bill was one of a small army of Aldersons who kept farm-life ticking over in a part of the dale-country where, quite often, t'clouds is mucky and summer may be nothing more than a good-natured wink between two long winters.

Said Bill, on one of my regular visits: "It's aw reet as lang as thou doesn't git snawed-up i'bed." I asked for an explanation. He said that when he was young and fit he usually left a small casement window open at night. One night, a lot of snow was delivered by a wind full of spite. "It came on such a whizziker," said Bill. "There was a big drift pointing up to the house. Snow came in at this window.

"Through t'neet I wasn't so hot in bed, so I covered missen up in t'clothes. And next morning, my sister opened t'room door – I wasn't wed then – and remarked: "Nay, what a mess!" His bedroom had a thick layer of snow. "Bed was covered. Snow was piled up on t'dresser. It had thawed on t'bed just where I had been laid.

 "I shouted to mi sister: 'Leave door oppen.' An' when I got up, I loped out o' bed into t'passage. I had nowhere to stand to get dressed. Bedroom was all covered wi' snaw. That's why I often say: 'It's not so bad if thou doesn't git snawed-up i' bed'." After breakfast, Bill had gone out to leuk t'sheep. "There was one place where t'snaw were so bad I had to go on my hands and knees."

The dalesmen spent some of the long June days digging peat. "We always had a peat-pot; it could be five or six foot deep. We opened it up by cutting a sod off t'top, and when we'd done, we put that sod back in t'bottom – we'd lain t'grund back – so it would be firm." The turves were spread to harden; then set up to dry in wind and sunshine. Some were raised in stacks for further drying.

"We'd cut some big flat peats and lap'em on top of a stack to turn t'weather. It was like roofing a house...At finish, I used to put 'em on a wall-top. There was a grand wall not so far away. I'd line yon wall wi' peat for maybe a quarter of a mile." The "peearts" were bagged and the bags stacked on a horse-drawn sled. "It was all down-bank to a peeart-'ouse."

The dalesfolk claimed that good peat warmed you twice, "yance on t'moor and yance when you sat beside a peat fire." The fireplaces at some of the farmhouses were huge. "When you were finishing of a night, at, say, five o'clock you'd back up a fire wi' plenty o'peats. Then you'd have it for t'night. You didn't want any more. And it'd get so hot, you could nearly roast a beast [bullock] on't."

Bill Alderson told me of a continuous round with sheep: the hard days attending to the lambing flocks; the summertime washing-days, when becks were dammed up and men stationed themselves in the pools to ruffle the wool of sheep thrown to them by their helpers. At haytime, the long-bladed scythe was being used. Hay was taken to the wintering sheep by creel, a wicker framework strapped to the back of a man, or in sacks, suspended from a Dales pony.

Such a pony was ready for general work on the dalehead farm at the age of three years. The farmer might first harness it to a sled. He then coaxed it through the difficult period of hauling a cart, which moved with a loud grating sound from the iron-rimmed wheels. The breaking-in operation must not be hurried. "It's nea use breakin' yan 'at's deeard."

A farmer who named a pony Chance explained to me that when he bought it "on t'chance" he was not sure of its capabilities. In the event, she was "a good 'un" - genial, good-tempered, easy-going. "You didn't worry when you saw kids going up to feed it." A farmer who bought "a wrang 'un" was in trouble. I heard of a horse that'd go backards afore it'd go forrards. We didn't know where we were going. If there had been a scar just behind us, it'd hev gone ower t'top."

Old ponies did not fade away. After seventeen or eighteen years of useful life they might be sold to the "knacker-fellow". One who bought a pony from a Swaledale farmer asked how long he might have before he had to pay for it. Said the farmer: "Thou can have as many days as thou likes; but neea neets!"

In some cases, the Dales pony, long considered as one of the family, was pensioned off, allowed to have peaceful days in the top pasture until "it got wearied, its eyes sunk – and t'farmer went up wi' a gun an' shot it."

As he is working with limestone, this waller is wearing rubber gloves to protect his hands.

Farmer at Whaw in Arkengarthdale – a tributary valley of Swaledale.

5

COURTSHIP AND MARRIAGE

In my long chat with Alf, I mentioned that I never motor through Carperby, in Wensleydale, without looking at the facade of the *Wheatsheaf* for a small notice recording that he and his bride spent their honeymoon here in 1941. "It was," said Alf, "a testing honeymoon. I hadn't a bean in those days." The work of tuberculin-testing cows was overdue. So he and his new wife Joan spent part of the time with the livestock. She kept the records. He injected the cows and called out their skin measurements.

They had been married in Thirsk; they arrived in Carperby after dark, and yet Mrs Kilburn and her niece Gladys were waiting with a hot meal – the first of many memorable meals. "The farmers were aghast that I should spend part of my honeymoon doing vet's work. Yet it was a very good honeymoon – and it was cheap."

Alf courted, won and wed Joan Catherine Danbury. He was a struggling vet, she was a secretary at Rymer's Mill – a corn mill – and, being pretty and vivacious, had a string of boyfriends. Going out with Joan was, for Alf, his first real romance. He was to describe in a book her small straight nose and a mouth turned up markedly at the corners, heralding a smile. Other features were blue eyes, arching brows and black-brown hair.

Highlights of the courtship were captured first in the books, then in cinema films. My favourite was the first film, where James's small Ford car needed a wheel-change, in pouring rain. The young vet was taking Helen on a first date, at a posh hotel. They went back to the Alderson farm to dry out, then resumed the journey. It turned out to be the wrong night for a dinner-dance.

In his authorised biography, Jim Wight records the true story of that soggy evening. It was Alf's first evening with Joan in the company of their friends. The Ford car ground to a halt on a flooded road, with water seeping through cracks in the floor.

The men in the party pushed the car clear of the water and re-started the engine. They returned to Kirkgate to dry out. With commendable persistency, they attended the dance – then returned to Kirkgate for drink, talk and to listen to some of Brian's entertaining tales.

A tender moment in the cinema film was when Helen brought in Dan, a family sheepdog which had a dislocated hip. James was about to call Siegfried to assist when she offered to help. She enjoyed working with animals. James invited Helen to join him at the local cinema. They sat in one of the courting seats – two seats, no arm between them – being, as it turned out, a week too soon for the film that had attracted them. "Next time," said Helen, amiably, "let's go for a walk." They did, filmwise, in Whitby.

When Freda and I were courting, we visited Whitby. We also had an unforgettable visit to the cinema to see *The Quiet Man*, based on a short story by Maurice Walsh. It was a wet day. The cinema was packed. Sodden clothes were draped on seat backs and along the front of the balcony. Spectacles steamed up. There was a hint of moisture in the beam of light from projector to screen. We viewed the film mistily.

Also nostalgic for me was a description in a Herriot book of afternoon tea at Helen's farm – and a sudden call for James to attend to a cow that had collapsed with "grass staggers". He injected a dose of magnesium. Before it had time to work, the cow stopped leg-thrashing. It was dead. I was to recall a springtime meal at Freda's farmhouse home. Dad, arriving late, popped a chilled orphan lamb in the oven for a minute or two to revive the luckless critter.

Dancing also formed part of my courtship. Years before, music at Dales dances had been provided by concertina "or maybe a fiddle" and it was not unknown for farmers' sons from the dalehead to arrive on

**The Wheatsheaf at Carperby,
where Alf and Joan Wight spent
their honeymoon in 1941.**

**Alf outside Thirsk parish church, where he and Joan were married.
(Yorkshire Evening Press)**

horseback, wearing breeches and leggings. Rabbit Pie Jimmy – so called because he was fond of singing a song about a pie – entertained one gathering with a musical item.

Freda and I went to "village hops" and also an annual Craven Tenant Farmers' ball in the Town Hall at Skipton. A Big Band played all the old familiar tunes. When we were not quick-stepping or foxtrotting to contemporary favourites, we went *Down the Strand*, sojourned at the *Old Bull and Bush* or proclaimed to the world in loud voices, while dancing, that *My Girl's a Yorkshire Girl – Yorkshire Through and Through.*

An orb set high up against the ceiling was composed of tiny mirrors; the orb revolved slowly and when a spotlight rested upon it, everything and everyone were covered with a moving pattern of colourful blobs that would have put a peacock's tail to shame.

Among the tenant farmers were families "off t'tops", blinking at the bright lights and the unaccustomed crowd of people. I saw grey-haired men in crow-black suits, their shirts with the old-fashioned "wing" collars, their footwear consisting of outmoded boots.

Young bucks set the fashion in dress suits and stimulated talk among the "wallflowers" [non-dancers] who remembered when Young Jack's father hadn't a penny to scratch his bottom on. Young George's grandfather was – well, you know...And looks were exchanged. The "you know" probably meant nothing more serious than being labelled a spendthrift and leaving a less than respectable sum in his will.

The courtship of Joan and Alf was similar to that of many others in rural Yorkshire. Visits to the 1s.9d seats in the cinema or a swirl at a dance hall were highlights. In a cash-strapped situation, courtship was mainly spent walking, hand in hand, a favourite area for our couple being Rievaulx Abbey. It was the height of the cinema-going craze. Alf and Joan, on the eve of their wedding, and also as a honeymoon couple, on their way to Carperby, patronised the Zetland cinema at Richmond. It was inexpensive – and cosy.

Alf's proposal of marriage to Joan had been made in the summer of 1941; she accepted, despite family concerns. Alf's parents also had objections to the marriage. The couple were undaunted and in due course a mellowing process developed on both sides. When, at 8 am on 5 November, 1941, James Alfred Wight married Joan Catherine Anderson Danbury, both sets of parents were absent.

Being a wartime wedding, it was austere. There was no heat in the grandiose church of St Mary's in Thirsk. Canon Young, who officiated, was seen to shiver with cold. Joan was "given away" by Fred Rymer, from the mill. Donald, the best man, handed the happy couple £5 as a wedding present and provided a champagne breakfast at 23 Kirkgate.

Alf and his bride had scarcely a penny in the world beyond that monetary present as he drove his beloved Joan across the vacant moors to Wensleydale. They reached their honeymoon quarters, *Wheatsheaf* at Carperby, after dark, yet Mrs Kilburn and her niece Gladys were waiting with a hot meal – the first of several memorable meals.

Two days of their five-day honeymoon were spent tuberculin-testing cattle, an irksome but necessary job. "The farmers were aghast that I should spend part of my honeymoon doing vet's work. Yet it was a very good honeymoon and it was cheap."

The operation, fictionalised, with the couple transformed as James and Helen, became the final sequence in the first cinema film to be based on the Herriot books. Helen closed the book in which the record of the cattle testing was recorded. She sauntered down the field towards a five-barred gate. James followed. They met up. Helen pushed back the shining dark hair from her forehead, caught his eye and smiled. He smiled back, with admiration. They kissed. And suddenly they – and the cinema audience – became aware of their setting: a glorious vista of dale and moor.

Donald was married in 1943. Two years later he and his wife moved out of Kirkgate. "Then we had the run of the place," said Jim. "The family just clattered about this enormous house. It was the surgery and living quarters – the whole thing in one. The walls were decked with incredible pictures, including *The Death of Nelson*."

In winter, much time was spent reading. Snow was expected, arrived and was promptly dug out. Alf soon realised that the climate in Yorkshire was much colder than in Glasgow. Spare time in summer might, in favourable weather conditions, be devoted to gardening.

One little-known Herriot story was told to me by Bill Shuttleworth, farmer of Earby, of happy memory. He occasionally called to see us at our home at Settle. Bill usually walked straight into the house. He would stand on the carpet before the living room fire and relate an entertaining tale, before departing as briskly as he had arrived.

Hearing that James Herriot was expected at Leyburn Sports, Bill and his wife attended. He arrived at the secretary's tent. "Where's Alf?" he demanded. The chief guest was somewhere on the showfield. Said Bill: "Put a message on the tannoy to say that an old friend has come to see him." They did. And Alf duly turned up at the tent.

He could not recall Bill or his wife. He was asked if he remembered his honeymoon at the *Wheatsheaf*, Carperby. Of course he did! Bill said, triumphantly: "You had an attractive, dark-haired wife. Me and my new wife were staying there at the same time. It was our honeymoon." At the mention of his dark-haired wife, Alf had smilingly pointed to Joan. After the passage of so many years, her hair was by no means as dark as it had been.

When, in 1942, Alf was serving in the R.A.F., part of the time in Scarborough, Joan moved to her parents' home. He rejoined her on his discharge. The children were born at "Sunnyside Nursing Home" – James Alexander (Jim) in 1943 and Rosemary Beatrice (Rosie) in 1947.

Hearing about Alf's courtship and marriage awakened memories of my own, which was a real Dales affair. Yorkshire courtship usually lasted for two to three years. My father told of a couple who had been "walking out" for 14 years when the young woman said to the man: "Isn't it about time we got wed?" He replied: "Who'd have us?"

Freda and I met on a bus. We had both been working late – she at Johnson and Johnson, the baby powder people who had a factory at Gargrave, me at the *Dalesman*. I slumped in my seat through boredom, only to perk up when Freda sat beside me. It was the only spare seat in the bus. I had seen Freda at dances. I wrote to her, suggesting another meeting. She agreed.

A bus timetable ruled our courtship, which was divided between Skipton and her family's remote farm. If I was visiting Freda, courting ended at precisely 9 pm with the arrival at the farmhouse gate of the last bus back to town. For dances, Mr Steele's taxi came into use. On one late night trip, pre-Christmas, he was so fatigued he stopped near a puddle, got out of the car and doused his face.

Freda's family had a stone-built farmhouse with an attractive porch. Rooms were accessed from a central passage. On my first visit, I attuned myself to paraffin lighting. It was wintertime. A lamp stood on the big table around which the diners sat.

The lamp flickered and went out part way through the first course which, this being a special day, consisted of salmon – straight from the tin, not mixed with breadcrumbs which was a common domestic economy in post wartime years. Knives and forks were laid aside as the lamp was dismantled, its wick trimmed, the glass cleaned.

We were into the sweet course, something with custard, when Dad – as he was known to everyone, including his wife – turned up. He was a small, lean man who in his positive manner and movement, and his taciturnity, typified a dale-country farmer. He had been assisting one of his dairy cows with a difficult birth.

Ignoring his seat by the table, he slumped in his cane chair at the fireside – the chair across the back of which was draped the fleece from a black sheep. Dad sighed. If he had put the same intensity into a stage sigh, he would have won a prize for drama. Said Mum, feelingly: "I wish I'd got that cold instead of Dad."

The so-called "front room", holding the better furniture, plus photographs and Victorian prints in antique frames, was mainly used by courting couples. Freda had three brothers and a sister. Her mother enjoyed courting nights and spent part of the evening with the current courting couple, keen to know what was going on in the outer world.

Martha, an ancient aunt of Dad, lived at a moorside farm near Thornton-in-Craven. We had a family gathering. Clad in Sunday best, she occupied a comfy chair with the relatives and friends forming an arc before her. There was no immediate reply when she was complimented on her ninetieth birthday.

Her response was, typically for a rural Yorkshirewoman, brief and spirited. She remarked: "I'll outlive t'lot of you!" It was followed by a sound like the movement of a rusty hinge. Aunt Martha was laughing.

On the farm, at lambing time, I toured the fields with Dad as he checked on the condition of his yows and their offspring. Weakly ones were brought to a croft near the farmhouse, where he might "keep an eye on them." I carried a new-born lamb across several fields, with the parent yow bleating as it followed me. What I remember, as a town lad, was the strong beating of the lamb's heart within a new, floppy body. Such strong heartbeats would enable it to get to its feet and suckle within a few moments of birth.

Freda and I met twice a week. Once, we strolled through a cemetery where some of the family had been laid to rest. One of the other graves bore the name of the deceased followed by the word "Resting". My dad had said he never did owt else!

THE MOORLANDERS

Donald Sinclair's practice covered an area from Helmsley to Hawes. With a base at Thirsk, it was natural that most calls came from the moorland bloc to the east, which – being almost fifty miles wide – was described by Alf as "a spacious, airy country of heather and deep gills." Jim observes that most of the published tales happened in and around Thirsk. The Moors were handy; the Dales lay over twenty miles away to the west.

Through *The Dalesman* I soon became aware of a distinctive moorland way of life. In the mid-1950s – James Herriot time – I visited Green End, Goathland, and sat beside one of the last turf-fires. Burning turf was a general custom which faded with the importation of coal. I called at Green End, having noticed a turf-stack in the yard. It would keep the kitchen fire glowing non-stop the winter through.

Do not confuse "greeaving" turf with peat-digging. Turf is merely topsoil after the ling has been burnt off. A turf fire burns strongly but slowly, throwing out a penetrating heat. It is more friendly and reliable than coal and does not clog the chimney with soot. The chimney at the farm I visited had not been swept within living memory.

Traditionally, the heather was burnt-off before a turf was cut by spade (either a cock or a hen spade). Firing the heather took place in late February and March. Then the moorland was dry. It was hoped to get the turves "rooked up" before haytime.

I watched the lady of the house make up the fire. Dark brown pieces of turf were banked up to a great height. Surely, she had extinguished the fire. A seepage of blue smoke was the first sign of life. Within twenty minutes there was a steady glow and such heat I moved my chair back

Alf with Tommy Masterman at Ampleforth. Tommy's bearded son Watson has a supporting role. (Jim Wight collection)

Lambing time at Kilburn. Alf is with the local shepherd John Stabler. (Jim Wight collection)

Alf with an array of cattle at
Wethercote Farm, Cold Kirby, where
conditions are frequently much
harsher than on the plains closer to
Thirsk. (Jim Wight collection)

several yards.

Alf doubtless sat beside one or two turf fires as he attended to the needs of moorland farmers. The villages on his list included Boltby, Kilburn and Coxwold. Whenever he reached the top of Sutton Bank, he spent a few minutes gazing at "the finest view in England". Jim was to observe in his biography: "A mile or two further east, he could look across thirty or forty miles of unbroken moorland towards the Yorkshire coast and the towns of Whitby and Scarborough."

Many of the farmsteads to which he was called lay at an elevation of around 800-ft. By and large, they were small family farms, roofed with red pantiles. From an early age, Jim and Rosie toured the farms with their father. Jim vividly recalls travelling in freezing-cold cars along incredibly rutted tracks. It was his job to open the gates. "You don't get that now, of course. Most farms have cattle grids and decent approaches."

At one farm there were seven gates across the approach track. They must be opened and closed on both the outward and return journeys, "making fourteen gate-opening operations in all." Most gates were falling to bits, being cobbled together with billy-band (baler twine).

When Rosie began to attend school at the age of five, she was concerned in case her father could not cope on the rounds without her. "We loved going with him on night calls. We'd hold torches while he calved cows and stitched up teats."

The Dales were notorious for snow but – as Jim was to write in the authorised biography of his father – the high ground of the Thirsk practice was just as bad. When it was raining in Thirsk, villages such as Cold Kirby or Old Byland on the top of the Hambleton Hills could be experiencing sweeping blizzards.

"Alf got to know, only too well, the high-pitched buzz of his car tyres as they spun wildly on the frozen roads or the sight of the exquisitely-shaped snow drifts sweeping across the road, beautiful but deadly as they relentlessly erased his tracks in the snow. Many times, as he struggled with tough cases on remote farms, he wondered whether he would be able to return home safely over the white, snowbound roads..."

Once, facing heavy rain as he drove up Sutton Bank, he stopped the car for a moment or two just below the summit of the road and watched snow powdering the moor-edge almost immediately above him. On a winter night, the headlamp beams picked up the form of a large stag. It leapt over the bonnet – to be lost to sight in darkness.

Jim Wight's career as a vet was spent in the Thirsk area, which takes in the Hambletons. Dad was aware that the land around Thirsk was so good for arable crops it was unlikely ever to be a country vet's paradise. "The fields had the wrong sort of green – turnip-tops and sugar-beet rather than grass. Vets don't make much out of sugar-beet."

Life on a moor-edge farm, where there was a goodly number of men, was hard on the womenfolk. The farmer's wife had the house to run, the clothes to wash, dry and iron, and food to bake to cater for appetites developed through hard physical toil. "A man who was set to muck out a foldyard by hand with a grype built up a tremendous appetite," said Jim.

He'd spoken to old ladies, farmers' wives, and heard when they'd cook five meals a day. "There'd be breakfast, with porridge and bacon and eggs. Then there'd be 10 o' clocks – or 'lowance, as they said. There was often a roast for dinner, which came at noon. There might be an afternoon break with apple pies, scones, sandwiches and cakes. At teatime, a 'fry-up' was appreciated. Supper followed in due course."

Alf Wight included this huge moorland block in Herriotshire, the area of Yorkshire which was of special interest. He got to know it well while travelling to and from the coast by other than the main roads. My introduction to the moorland way of life came when I visited Goathland.

Rievaulx Abbey, one of the best-known features in the
huge moorland block that forms part of 'Herriotshire'.

Opposite:

Top: Typical farmstead of the North York Moors in Bilsdale.

Bottom: Thatched cottages at Rievaulx.

This quiet little village would, through the television series *Heartbeat*, develop into a tourist hotspot. Even now, when I half-close my eyes, I can recapture the delight of a breezy, russet, mid-1950s village. Goathland was scented by an exquisite tang compounded of heather and peat.

Some of the moorland sheep were already losing their appetites for grass and young heather shoots. Visitors fed them on unsheeplike food ranging from sandwiches to liquorice allsorts. The sheep mobbed picnic parties, greeted the arrival of every tourist bus and the regular red-sided service buses. Some sheep clambered into cars, the doors of which had been left open.

I was introduced to Matilda, an old and tattered "Swaledale cross". She was thin in t'wool and loose in t'teeth. She was known to accept such varied food as scones and apple peelings. Matilda dropped and reared her lambs in the shadow of the churchyard wall.

An insight into the traditions of the North East Moors was given to me by R W Crosland, who lived at Hutton-le-Hole. He mentioned to me the extreme isolation of some of the farms. There may be a mile or more of heather between such places and their nearest neighbours. From some of the farms no other house could be seen. At one house, five miles from anywhere, Crosland was told that the children never went to school. "We didn't; and ours don't. How can they?"

To many people, a small cottage – even one of a row of three, built for mine-workers, tucked away in a dale within a dale, with the moor-gate a mere fifty yards away – is remote. The travel writer John Hillaby, whose Yorkshire home this was, smiled at the idea. He was a man of "deserts", either dry or soggy. In some respects, Rosedale was not remote enough, though it offered sanction and such peace that he might – as he expressed it – hear a sheepdog break wind in Farndale.

I drove to his home in Rosedale from Hutton-le-Hole. Signs warning of the horrors of Rosedale Bank gave me a sense of foreboding. With its maxium gradient of 1 in 2 ½, it is claimed by some to be the steepest stretch of road in England. John Hillaby said: "I heard of a man who walked down t'Bank and suddenly found he was looking "straight into mi wellies."

At the peak of the day, John Hillaby was at one of the Rosedale pubs. He had already been for a five-mile walk, and had done his daily stint at the typewriter. I knew him quite well, having travelled with him – as a reader of his books – through Britain. I asked him about his moorside home. John had bought the place from a publican who had used it at week-ends. "It occurred to me early that it would be best to try and make the cottage blend into the moorscape."

Our talk was interrupted by a crash from the kitchen. I took the sound to be a manifestation of gravity. John said: "That's the hob, by the way." He was referring to one of the "wee folk" of the Moors.

John and his second wife had transformed the garden. "It's not a big plot: no more than sixteen paces from the front door to the front gate. What is the moor but peat? I got about three or four loads of peat and eventually the garden's acidity was near to that of the Common which lies immediately above the cottage. The obvious plants to encourage were heathers."

John spoke at length about the ubiquitous nature of the moor-jocks, as he called the local sheep. When ravenous, they were inclined to invade the dale. That morning, at about seven o' clock, John looked out of his cottage window and saw twenty or thirty "jocks" cheerfully champing his precious collection of heathers – a collection he had built up over a number of years to provide continuous flowering for months on end.

John was often solitary, never lonely. The moor birds entertained him. He described the golden plover as "a strange, lonely bird with a solitary little call, *tee-oo-oo.*" Next to return to the moors was the pee-wit [lapwing]. "After that we have the symbol of the moors – the curlew. It floats in – and 'float' is the word; you can sometimes see birds rising on the thermals,

Hutton-le-Hole, one of the most attractive villages of the North York Moors, is noted for its folk museum.

moving from one spire of upcurrents to another, sweeping in..."

One snowtime, red grouse descended to the rough pasture behind the back door, announcing themselves with "that clattery whirr, an unfailing *diminuendo* that ends in a staccato *go-back, go-back, go-back-back-back.*"

Some of the flockmasters – those who did not keep their gates and walls in good order – were termed freebooters. This was John Hillaby's polite word for "fodder thieves". I appreciated his problem and was much too polite to ask him if he had considered fencing the garden against the sheep.

I had a brief chat about farming with Bert Frank, one of the supporters of what has become a celebrated folk museum. He told me that at haytime, the farmers did not want for labour – if they provided barrels of ale. Methodism had been established in Rosedale. Not every farmer would like to pander to the "baser appetites". Strong drink was to a Methodist of that time "the devil in suspension". Bert has heard it said that some miners spent so much money on drink that, at home, the family had to drink their tea out of jam jars.

I got to know the North York Moors in a way that would have appealed to Alf – trudging along the Coast to Coast route, as devised by Alfred Wainwright. It was springtime, 1995, when with three friends, after the total of 12,000-ft of climbing in Lakeland and a pounding on miles of hard road in the Plain of York, we reached the north-east moorland, which is thatched by 100,000 acres of ling. Alf considered that the motif for the North York Moors is distance and heather.

We entered Scugdale, then crossed Carlton and Cringle Moors, viewing the conical form of Roseberry Topping, locally claimed to be "the highest hill in all Yorkshire." We sipped coffee in Lord Stones, a refreshment place built into a hillside. As we traversed a moorland trod beyond, there was the novelty of being greeted by the pilot of a passing hang-glider. The Wainstones broke the skyline.

At Urra Moor, 1,489-ft, we were on the highest point of the Coast to Coast. Heathery vistas were relieved by standing stones. It snowed when, after following a green track on which a railway line had been set, we came within sight of the remote *Lion Inn*. From across the chilled moor came the melancholic double-notes of a golden plover.

On to Eskdale, paying our respects to Young and Old Ralph and to Fat Betty (moorland crosses). On our last day, we had a stiff climb from Grosmont to the moors. The route eased off as we strode to Littlebeck and on through a swing gate marked Falling Foss into sunlit woodland.

There was a quick slog over Greystone Hills and a final tract of moorland before Hawsker. A path between rows of caravans led us to the edge of the cliffs, where we came under the solemn gaze of fulmar petrols and herring gulls. We made the steep descent in Robin Hood's Bay to where a flow tide smacked its lips against stone – and our boots.

Lying to the south of the Moors are the Yorkshire Wolds, a broad crescent of chalk, extending visually from Humber to Flamborough Head. It had its own special type of farming – and its specialist vets. Irene Megginson, a much-loved *Dalesman* correspondent, kept the Wolds in the picture for us.

She mentioned that fothering and tending calves were constant jobs. "There's usually a calf with feeding problems, and the vet might be called with life-saving medications fetched from Driffield. Modern farmers have to be handy in giving injections which are a great advancement on the old 'fellon drinks'.

With road travel difficult in winter, a farmer kept a good supply of remedies. Irene remembered Stockholm tar, linseed oil, Epsom salts and packets of colic drinks. They were tiny coloured glass bottles containing various potions and a large green bottle of "white oils". "Some, with grubby labels, could have been almost anything!"

Also kept on the shelf were a box of coloured rings for identifying hens'

Features of the Coast to Coast Walk:

Memorial to Henry Jenkins in the churchyard at Bolton-on-Swale.

Signpost in woodland near Richmond.

Lord Stones Café – patronised by Coast to Coasters.

Gritstone outcrops on the Moors:

One of the spectacularly eroded Bridestones near the Forest Way.

Over: The Wainstones, which break the skyline from several viewpoints.

ages, a pot egg for encouraging reluctant layers, tiny long-necked bottles for dosing lambs and a jar of sulphur for use in hen huts. "These were a great trial at spring-cleaning time. All had to be dusted. Clean papers must be put underneath, with no time to read more than the headlines."

When Alf first came to Yorkshire, he was well out of sight of the North Sea and far too busy with his veterinary duties to take time off to watch waves break their backs on sandy beaches or against formidable cliffs. His introduction came when he was called up for service in the RAF. For six months he was billeted, marched and drilled at Scarborough.

His chief remembrance was of fresh air – and lots of it. There was no respite from a north-easter. The RAF had taken over the *Grand Hotel*. When Alf and others were on fire-picket, they occupied the towers at the corners of the massive building. Peacetime memories at Scarborough would include languid days at the Cricket Festival.

In a book of Yorkshire memories, Alf was to recall when Richie Benaud hit five sixes in succession off Roy Tattersall. Alf could recite the names of cricket personalities as in a litany – Bradman, Miller, Harvey, Hutton, Compton, May...

I told Alf my favourite Yorkshire cricket story. It had been related to me by Freddie Trueman. On the first day of a county match, Yorkshire versus Glamorgan, at Harrogate, an old-age pensioner went along to pay for his membership subscription. He and the secretary chatted about the good weather.

Said the secretary: "You'd have thought there'd be more people in the ground on a lovely day like this." The pensioner remarked: "I wouldn't worry; it'll fill up after lunch." The secretary asked why this should be. Said the pensioner: "It's half-day closing at Pateley Bridge."

Alex Taylor, a friend since their Glasgow days, and at the time a prominent member of the Marquis of Normanby's estate staff, made it possible for himself and the Wight family to spend a night or two in a seaside – literally seaside – cottage at Runswick Bay. Thatched and white-painted, it stood out even among a cluster of red-pantiled buildings.

Alf excitingly recalled when he would awake at night to the thump of waves breaking against an adjacent sea wall. Anther coastal settlement that seemed to cling desperately to a Yorkshire cliffscape was Robin Hood's Bay, where Alf had his first-ever family holiday after spending every night on call for eleven years.

Alf's introduction to the Yorkshire coast came when he was called up for RAF service and was based at Scarborough. Places that soon became familiar to him included:

Whitby, with its Caedmon memorial in the churchyard at the top of the celebrated steps.

Filey – a tractor is drawing a coble.

North Landing, Flamborough – and its colourful fishing boats.

WORDS AND PICTURES

Raised in the city of Glasgow, Alf's first impression of Yorkshire had been as a "stodgy, uninteresting place – rural in parts, perhaps, but dull." He made this confession reflectively in a big picture book entitled *James Herriot's Yorkshire*. His discovery of the Dales had begun when he motored from Thirsk to Leyburn to assist Frank Bingham. "I suddenly found myself in wonderland."

It was Mrs Herriot – er, Joan Wight – who encouraged Alf to jot down his memories of a vet's life in Yorkshire. He had the usual early frustrations of an author, not least the style to be adopted. Alf was "turned fifty" before he put pen to paper, referring to events that had occurred many years earlier.

It was Joan who specified Michael Joseph as a possible publisher. Several years went by before the manuscript of Alf's first book arrived on the desk of an agent and was passed on to Michael Joseph for scrutiny. In that first book, *If Only They Could Talk*, which was published in 1970, he related incidents from his experiences as a vet in rural Yorkshire and his comparatively short service in the RAF.

The story began with the young vet's arrival at Darrowby, a composite town, "a bit of Thirsk, something of Richmond, Leyburn and Middleham, and a fair chunk of my imagination." The human interest was mainly in the varying relationships of the brothers Sinclair, who were given those Wagnerian names of Siegfried and Tristan.

Sales were steady until, deviously, the wife of Tom McCormack, chief executive of St Martin's Press, New York, recognised Alf's storytelling talent and the book's potential as a best-seller. McCormack, on a visit to London, was keen to acquire something spectacular that would bolster the declining fortunes of his company.

He was handed a copy of Alf's book. For an American accustomed to chunky books, this relatively small book, by an unknown author who was a vet in Yorkshire, had little appeal. A copy was handed to him and, being courteous, he slipped it into his briefcase. In due course, and for several months, it lay unread on a table at his New York home.

Tom's wife picked it up and read it with amusement and excitement. Her advice to Tom, the big executive, was: "You gotta read this…" He did. But differently. He incorporated the first two books, plus three additional chapters, in a single volume. The American reader would have the customary handful.

The collective title – *All Creatures Great and Small* – was another vital breakthrough and was an American adaptation of *Ill Creatures Great and Small* originally suggested to Alf by his daughter Rosie. This was the apt second line of a popular children's hymn written in Ireland by Cecil Frances Alexander. Alf's writings would benefit hugely from other lines in that first evocative verse of *All Things Bright and Beautiful*.

The book was published in America in November 1972, to a deafening silence. Then a reviewer in the *Chicago Tribune* wrote about it with enthusiasm for its style and content, observing: "If there is any justice, this will become a classic of its kind…"

When I met Alf at his Thirlby home, I mentioned this phase of his life. He said: "I don't know what the attraction was for the Americans but they definitely fell for it. It became a bestseller over there, you know. The British publisher became aware of the possibilities – and that was it!" But for this, "my books would have faded away as, sadly, do much better books. I was limping along."

Jim said his father was inclined to conceal the identity of some of his characters by altering sexes. The tales were based upon fact that was then embellished. What he wrote about Skeldale House and about the

Alf types as Joan reads and watches television. This is how he wrote all his books.
(Terence Spencer, Life magazine)

two Farnon brothers – not forgetting the pint pot – was as it happened.

At *The Dalesman* we applauded a book written by a vet. James Herriot had provided a story that every Yorkshire farmer would enjoy – an account of a young vet's first year out of college, grappling with the problems of a Yorkshire farming area. "The experiences are lively, unpredictable, and often very earthy, and they tell of days before all the modern drugs and chemicals and mechanical aids of today were available."

Every vet had his hypodermic syringe and that gave him an air of authority with the farmer if not with the animals. There were grim, startling and hilarious moments among the farm folk as among the animals. No one quite knew what a slip of paper with the words: "Dean, 3 Thompson's Yard. Old dog ill" could lead to – but it was certainly not peace and quiet.

A book by James Herriot was notable for its well-drawn, usually larger-than-life characters, a light and amusing touch and restrained but appealing descriptive passages of landscape, weather and farmsteads. It was good writing in every respect. By the 1980s, books bearing the name James Herriot had been translated into every major language. A Japanese version was available. Fifty million copies of Herriot titles were sold in 20 countries.

I eventually discussed with Jim his forthcoming book about a famous father. At that stage he had written well over 100,000 words. Donald Sinclair, alias Siegfried, was featured strongly, being "probably the pivotal character in the Herriot books." When the idea of writing the book first occurred to Jim, he consulted his father's manuscripts for 1963-4. Donald was the person running strongly through all of them. "He was a likeable man, especially to women, but eccentric, unpredictable and virtually impossible to work with."

Invited to spend a week in America, Alf rode a wave of goodwill and returned to Yorkshire – knackered. With millions of copies of his books being sold, he had a three-week tour of America in the summer of 1973. When a book-signing session was held in New York, some fans arrived with copies of the books and their pets! He had huge earnings in the United States and in this country; and almost as huge demands from the Income Tax authority. For many years he was not as wealthy as people imagined.

The Herriot tales were to be given pictorial treatment through the cinema and television. Two cinema films based on the Herriot books and released to great box office success in the mid 1970s were *All Creatures Great and Small* and *It Shouldn't Happen to a Vet*. Both films were sponsored by *Readers' Digest*.

The first-named was "shot", initially to Alf's disappointment, on the North York Moors. He would have preferred the Yorkshire Dales but applauded the result. The part of James was played by Simon Ward. Anthony Hopkins, as Siegfried, captured his moments of wry humour and abrasive manner. Liza Harrow, as Helen, provided the love interest.

James was filmed arriving at York railway station. He caught a 1930s-style bus – not unlike the one which I booked for my wedding to Freda! – and traversed a moorland road before setting him down in a picturesque spot – Old Malton, which also featured in the wedding sequel.

Donald Sinclair (right), alias Siegfried - 'probably the pivotal character in the Herriot books.'

Donald with his wife Audrey. In 1945, they moved from Kirkgate to Southwoods Hall.

Having arrived in Darrowby, James headed for the vet's house. That first cinema film featured a fine old house in Houndgate, Pickering. During the period they were in occupation, a caller who rang the bell might be greeted by five lively dogs. The rooms of this attractive old house had been given the Thirties look.

In real life, Arthur Magson, aged 80, looked after the garden. He came closest to weeping when the film-makers brought in loads of weeds, including nettles, for he had just set out the three-quarter acre garden, which was immaculate. For several hectic weeks, actors spoke their lines, cameras turned and meals were prepared for about seventy people. Then all became tranquil again. And the garden was restored to its tidy state.

Alf Wight himself had rung the bell at Houndgate, presenting a copy of one of his books to Joan, Mary and Muriel Robertson, the owners of the hall. In the book, which he had signed, was a personal message: "With deepest gratitude for housing my creation."

I visited the house as the 1976 heatwave entered its third weary week. The car was oven-hot and the pavement in Houndgate came close to blistering my feet. The hall itself was cool, quiet, elegant. I was shown around a building in which a Medical Officer of Health – their grandfather, Dr D W Robertson – had brought up sixteen children.

The side of the house facing Houndgate – seen in the opening sequence of the film, as James Herriot arrives to assume work – had been painted a brilliant white which, the stonework being sandstone, was beginning to assume a honeyed appearance. The outside also appeared in a later stage where James and Helen, having been married, saw from a taxi the wall-plate indicating that James had been made a partner in the veterinary firm.

Worked into the plot, via the book, was the incident when Herriot was summoned to attend to a calf with a broken leg. On another occasion, he – with Helen's help – attended to a dog with a dislocated hip. They

During the shooting of the second cinema film in 1976. Left to right: John Alderton (who played the main role), Joan (Alf's wife), Liza Harrow (Helen), Alf. (Jim Wight collection)

Alf and Basil Aylward, the veterinary adviser for It Shouldn't Happen to a Vet.
(Jim Wight collection)

Opposite: The first episode in the new television serial All Creatures Great and
Small – January 1978. Left to right: Robert Hardy as Siegfried Farnon,
Christopher Timothy as James Herriot, Paul Luty as Bert Sharpe. (BBC)

were drawn to each other by mutual concern, then by mutual love.

The second film, *It Shouldn't Happen to a Vet*, shot in the Dales in 1975, was premiered in the springtime of the following year. John Alderton played the part of James and Colin Blakely was Siegfried. Lisa Harrow – Helen in both films – was said to bear a marked resemblance to Joan, Alf's wife, in her younger years. Jim, in his authorised biography, mentioned that Alf, having read the scripts, wanted the peaks and troughs of Siegfried's character to be smoothed out.

In 1977, Alf became a world-wide celebrity, via BBC Television. A series of half-hour programmes, based on the books, were projected as ninety episodes over a spell of twelve years. The now familiar title of *All Creatures Great and Small* was used. Herriotshire, its characterful folk and long-suffering animals, were transmitted into living rooms throughout the world.

The series was introduced with snatches of film that featured a moorland road with a watersplash, traversed by the famous old Austin 7; the aforementioned car crossing a hump-backed bridge at Langthwaite and, within the car, smiling and chatting, sat the two major characters – Christopher Timothy as James Herriot and Robert Hardy as Siegfried.

Supporting roles included Peter Davison as Tristan. Carol Drinkwater played the part of Helen in thirty-six episodes from 1978 until 1985. The role was taken over by Lynda Bellingham.

I photographed Christopher Timothy at Marsett on a day when filming had been delayed because a local sow would not farrow on cue! I watched love bloom in Wensleydale as the BBC recorded yet another instalment.

Arriving in the village of Askrigg on a May morning, when the dale was being sun-baked, I found everyone panting in the unaccustomed heat. Through the good offices of the producer, Bill Sellers, I had arranged to watch the cast and technicians of *All Creatures Great and Small* at work.

No head turned as I passed through a cordon of James Herriot fans keen to see the celebrities. We had Tender Romance as John McGlynn "warmed up some old broth" [returned to a former acquaintance, under a spreading chestnut tree]. Background noises led to problems for the sound-recordist. Rooks nesting in a lofty tree must have reached an emotional crisis for their calls were continuous, deafening.

I chatted with Christopher Timothy over lunch in the caterers' bus, one of a small fleet of specialist vehicles parked on the cobbles near Askrigg Church. He mentioned that in the Herriot books little or nothing is written about James. "Yet we have plenty of descriptions of Siegfried, Tristan and Helen. I had to take what little there is and fit a character to it. I was pleased when Jim Herriot, in his book about Yorkshire, considered I'd done this well. It was more luck than judgement."

His favourite Dales story was of the time when Robert Hardy, Peter Donaldson and he – the three principal players in the Herriot story – were supposed to be leaving the "vet's house" in Askrigg, say cheerio to each other and go their separate ways. "About 300 people who were mainly foreign visitors, were watching us make the film. The production assistant was being gentle with them.

"When we were still inside the front door, I heard 'Camera – sound – rolling – and ACTION'. We opened the front door to absolute silence. All the traffic had been stopped. Then across the front of the house walked a woman carrying two shopping baskets. She was dressed in a costume that was certainly applicable to the period.

"I heard 'CUT' and saw the production assistant going across to the lady to ask her if she would mind holding back while the scene was shot. The lady said, very loudly: 'I've got my bloody life to lead, you know.' And, of course, there was no answer to that. It was her village, not ours."

The watersplash between Swaledale and Arkengarthdale that featured in the opening sequence of All Creatures Great and Small.

A car of the same period as the Austin 7 used in the watersplash scene.

Christopher Timothy takes a break from filming.

Robert Hardy, one of the three principal players in the Herriot story.

Linda, who took over the role of Helen from Carol Drinkwater, told me this was her second Herriot series. "It's lovely for me to have an important part in a successful series." Until Herriot entered her life, she had never been to the Dales, though she had read the books about the famous vet. And, of course, she had seen the films. "I had not realised from those films how big and rolling the Dales country really is. I had tended to see it in Postman Pat terms – much smaller than reality."

Jeremy Summers, in production, mused: "The Herriot books have affected so many people. The author sat in his bath one day and thought: 'I'll write down all my Dales memories'. His books had benefited Publishers, Hoteliers, Garage Proprietors, Shopkeepers. Us!" I left him to his complex jig-saw of dialect and tasks with the confidence that when the series was projected the cawing of the rooks would not be jerky, there would be no unseemly reflections in the house windows – and no extraneous traffic noises."

The BBC needed horned cattle for filming *All Creatures Great and Small*, yet most of the remaining Dales cows had been de-horned, a fashion that had begun in the 1950s. A herd of the old-fashioned horned type was located at West Park, Baldersdale. These Shorthorns, grazing herby ground, had once yielded rich milk that was made into butter and cheese. The mother of the farmer, Thomas Birkett, had a considerable reputation for making the Cotherstone variety which vied in quality and digestibility with Wensleydale cheese.

With the co-operation of the farmer, the BBC arranged for several cows to be transported to open common near the *Punch Bowl* inn, Swaledale. Christopher Timothy or Robert Hardy invariably had a hand up the backside of a Birkett cow when the scriptwriter decreed there should be a difficult birth!

Visiting West Park in late summer, 1979, I found cattle dispersed in a way common in olden time. I patted a white Shorthorn which was now thirteen years old and had delivered eleven calves. My stroll through large, well-drained fields, looking at old-style animals, was a memorable experience.

Young stock occupied a huge pasture near the farm. In another field lay the milk cows. One or two beasts had down-curving horns. There was a notion in the Dales that this betokened a beast of a beefy type. The next field held three dried-off cows and, beyond, was a field of bullocks. In the last good field, just short of the moor, were in-calf heifers and stirks. In one of the buildings I came under the unblinking gaze of a fine bull.

Through television, the characters of the Herriot books entered our living rooms. Eventually, we seemed to know the denizens of Skeldale House, Darrowby, as well as the members of our own family. There was the young vet, James Herriot; his wife Helen; the irascible Siegfried Farnon and his wayward younger brother Tristan; plus a severe-looking but basically kindly housekeeper – and the unruly mob of assorted dogs.

Jeremy Summers, director of scenes from All Creatures Great and Small.

The Herriot Season was spread over thirteen weeks a year. Each episode began with a lively tune and film sequences shot in the dale country, heralding yet another episode in the Herriot saga. For fifty minutes, the characterful folk of the dale-country, their farms and domestic animals, performed their parts against a backdrop of greystone buildings and the long, lean Pennine ridges. (A few years before, we had been similarly entranced by the activities of doctors at the fictitious Tannochbrae, in *Doctor Finlay's Casebook*).

On a sunny day in 1979, driving along a moor road connecting

**The three-storey house in Askrigg that became
Skeldale House in the television series.**

Wensleydale with Swaledale, via the quaintly-named Oxnop, I found
myself on part of a film set. BBC Television was shooting sequences
for another series of programmes based on the tales of James Herriot.
I joined a small group of holidaymakers who brought me up-to-date on
the filming plans for the day.

Kit Calvert, of Hawes, was present. With his granddaughter he had
brought along Dolly, her pony, to be used as an "extra". Up a field, and
over a wall, came Christopher Timothy – the James Herriot of the films
– now almost fully recovered from a damaged leg that had given him a
limp in the previous series.

The lean lands of the Pennines were photogenic. We were able to recall some of the superficially hard, abrasive Dales farmers, especially the man who had a bull suffering from sunstroke and was relieved that the treatment was not some fancy potion but water, played on the animal from a hose. It was *his* water. Surely the bill from the vet would not be heavy!

The owner of a pig with a boil on its face must have derived wry amusement from the unsuccessful attempts to capture the ferocious animal for treatment. It was left to Tristan, the younger brother of Siegfried, to effect a cure – by losing his temper and chasing the pig in darkness, causing it to brush against a wall and burst the boil.

We think of the young vet's encounter with a farmer who had a cupboard laden with home-made wines of every type; he became merry – and was then summoned to a farm owned by devout Methodists, where under disapproving stares he attended to a calving. The 1930s were the lean years for Dales farming, as for veterinary surgeons.

The film *All Creatures Great and Small* gave us some splendid contrasts. We met wealthy and peke-struck Mrs Pumphrey and her obese, under-exercised, lethargic Tricki-woo. (Unknown to the proud owner and, indeed, to cinema-goers, one course of treatment was boisterous exercise with the vet's dogs, plus a few rat bites. The peke was returned home – to a welcoming gathering of humans and yet more rich food).

The television stars were well disposed towards the spectators. Over recent years, Robert Hardy, Peter Davison, Carol Drinkwater and Christopher Timothy, though strictly off-comers, charmed Dalesfolk and visitors alike, signing autograph books and chatting about their work. They even took part in a charity cricket match at Askrigg.

THE LATTER DAYS

When I met Alf Wight, towards the end of 1989, he said: "I'm naturally a pretty retiring bloke and I found I was being crushed down by publicity. I thought that the only way to get rid of this was to stop writing. And I did stop." He also discontinued writing for television. "I thought that when the story had reached the point when I went off to the war, it was a nice 'high' to end on. I had loved the television series; they took in so much of the Dales scenery."

Alf settled down to being a vet, "which, of course I was, 99 per cent of the time. My writing has been that much of my life (an inch, indicated by this thumb and forefinger). I'm not an author at all. If anyone criticises me as an author, I say: 'Well, I'm not an author. I'm a vet who scribbled for half an hour after his work at night.'"

The BBC were keen for him to resume his television association and, of course, his publishers were keen to have more books. When it was pointed out to him that there is little or no decent family viewing "on the box", he allowed more of his work to be used on the now ubiquitous television.

"They re-started production – and were soon running out of material. I wrote down more recollections for them." This re-awakened a feeling for writing that had been dead for a few years. He gave the BBC some storylines, with "little bits of dialect", to keep them going. "I was afraid of it being a big anti-climax but once this got started then I began filling in. I can see that one of these days I'll have another book."

A shopkeeper I met at Leyburn was wondering where all the day-trippers had gone. The market square looked dead, like the film set for

High Noon. I suggested that as the summer of 1998 had been almost continuously wild and wet, many of the tourists had not even set off from home.

There is a fickle element in tourism, which is a relatively modern phenomenon, in the way it caters for vast numbers of people. Yet many people still feel a warm glow around the heart when they think of James Herriot and his Yorkshire Dales – especially the Dales before the outbreak of war in 1939 brought about profound social changes.

Americans who turned up at the vet's surgery in Thirsk asked when a new book would be published. The American interest, it will be recalled, had been almost entirely responsible for the success of his first book. The Americans were coming in droves.

"Even though I am retired as a vet, I go down and see them at the surgery. There may be 150 lined up on a Friday. It used to be nearly every day, and then I cut it down to Wednesday and Friday. Now it's just the one day." He never bought or sold books. "We have a wonderful little bookshop in Thirsk. It is run by an American. A Texan. He keeps a good stock."

Alf's love of the Dales led him to buy a cottage in West Scrafton, Coverdale. He contrasted Leyburn of the early war years with that of today. "Visiting the town nowadays, we can hardly find space to park the car. It's so busy – so full of trippers. Leyburn has wonderful shops and cafes. What a difference!" He spent many a relaxing time at his Coverdale cottage, visiting it at all times of the year and in all weathers, going for long walks with the dogs in air scented by damp peat.

A J Brown, who wrote extensively about Yorkshire, considered that Coverdale comes near to being the ideal dale of one's dreams. "It is deep and quiet, remote and yet reasonably accessible, flanked by high hills at the dalehead and graced by verdant pasture-lands in the lower reaches of the river Cover...The whole dale is sprinkled with soothing and suggestive placenames – Woodale, Fleensop, Gammersgill,

Widdiman Pasture, Caldbergh and Coverham."

Jim relates that one late October, when sleet was falling, his father met a farmer whose clothes were partly covered by a hessian sack and whose feet were set in torn wellingtons. They chatted as they took shelter in an outbuilding. The farmer, who recognised the visitor, observed: "You're not just having a bit of a holiday up here, like?" Alf said: "Yes, just a nice break from the practice."

The farmer, who had a hard life, was bringing in some cows for milking. "He looked at my dad for a while and, knowing he had made money as an author and could relax on sun-drenched beaches in exotic locations, asked: why did you come here?"

The Dales farmers have prospered, though they are unlikely to admit it. A land agent said: "They used to come down in the war and say 'I've got a form; what shall I do with it?' We dealt with them, but by degrees they got to know every subsidy that was going and how to claim it. They have got their cars. There was hardly a car in the district up to the war – very few anyway. They bicycled or walked or went by train.

The hill farming grant was of great importance, providing the head of money to put up new buildings, to cover the cost of installing electricity, to improve water supplies and also to modernise the farmhouses. The old "black ranges" were succeeded by the AGA or Raeburn stoves. The old farmhouse was, on the whole, warm and dry, with a fire maintained throughout the year for cooking, heating water as well as infusing some heat into large, cold rooms.

"I've lived to see the farmers flourishing. Where there were two horses there is now probably three tractors and a Land Rover – and a private car." They are highly mechanised. At Keld, in Swaledale, a friend thought hard and long when I asked him who had the first tractor in the upper dale. Then he thought it might have been Percy Metcalfe, of Crackpot Hall, a "lile grey Fergie" he bought from Prestons of Bainbridge. And that was after the war.

My meeting with Alf Wight, alias James Herriot, at his Thirlby home took place shortly after he had retired from a vet's life. He had a heap of "back correspondence" to deal with; he was also trying to keep up with his writing. "I haven't a routine. In the lovely sunshine of last summer I went out – gardening and walking."

After our morning chat, he intended to walk with one of his oldest friends who had moved from Glasgow to a home in the North Riding. "It's very gradual walking. He and I are of the same age. We just walk and chat and put the world to rights." He sometimes sat at his word processor and thought of his arrival in these parts, fifty years before. "I write when I feel like it. I do a little bit at a time. I am finding, once again, that writing's fun..."

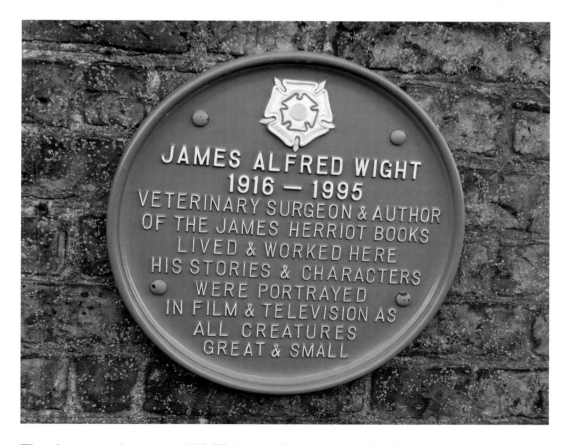

The plaque on the front of 23 Kirkgate, Thirsk – now The Herriot Centre.

Alf was diagnosed with prostate cancer. He underwent treatment in the local hospital but died at his home in Thirlby, with his family around him, on February 23, 1995. He was seventy-eight years of age. Joan survived him for several years and was in her eighties when she died.

On the winter day in 1999 when I met Jim Wight, son of Alf, the sun rose spectacularly as I was crossing the fertile vale east of Ripon. A gleaming orb had the sky to itself and tinted the landscape with gold. At Thirsk, the strengthening sunlight gilded St Mary's and the rows of gargoyles in the form of fearsome beasts. By now the sun was peering over ancient roofs as though eager to consult the clock tower set in a cobbled market place. I was in the heart of Herriotshire.

But for the cars, the town looked very much as it did when I explored it half a century before and when Alf Wight was making his rounds as a vet with an occasional sortie into the Pennine dales. I sipped tea in a cafe that had a see-through bakery at the back. Beyond the Darrowby Arms lay Kirkgate. My eyes quested for the elegant form of No 23, once the home and workplace of Alf.

No 23 Kirkgate, Thirsk, is now The Herriot Centre, furnished as it was when the celebrated vet lived and worked here. It also brings into sharp focus the personalities of the time, notably Donald Sinclair, the major figure in Alf's professional life. Donald Sinclair was never underhand. He always provided a square deal.

Just before Alf died, Jim asked him how he had managed to work with such a man for so many years. It must have been trying. Alf said: "I'll tell you this - he never stabbed me in the back." They remained close friends. And, as Alf said to his son Jim: "Where else could I have met such a man to put in my stories?"

Jim recalls: "Until a few days before Dad's death, he refused to give in – remaining determinedly mobile by walking around the house and garden every day...If ever a man fought cancer with fortitude, it was my father...If my father had a gravestone, I would inscribe upon it the advice that we, as his younger colleagues, heard from him time and time again: 'It's not what you do, it's the way that you do it.'"

On the day following Alf's death, and to keep a promise made by him to his old veterinary school, part of the University of Glasgow, Jim was present at the official opening of a new James Herriot Library,

Alf was cremated. On the suggestion of Rosie, his daughter, his ashes were scattered at the top of the Whitestone Cliffs which had formed the backdrop of much of his life. A commemorative tree was planted near his former home. Almost two thousand people attended a memorial service in York Minster. And, of course, there was a heartfelt rendering of Mrs Alexander's children's hymn, from the first verse of which had been drawn titles for Alf's best-known books:

All things bright and beautiful,

All creatures great and small;

All things wise and wonderful,

The Lord God made them all.

In Herriot's Yorkshire...

Askrigg. A notable Wensleydale village with a 13th century church and a cross on a cobbled market place. Alf had Askrigg in mind when he thought of the fictitious Darrowby. The facade of a prominent local building became Skeldale House in the BBC television series.

Carperby. Alf and Joan, after their wedding at Thirsk, went to the cinema and spent two nights of their honeymoon at the *Wheatsheaf*, sleeping in an old-fashioned brass bedstead. The two days were spent mainly in tuberculin-testing and recording cattle.

Coverdale. A captivating, tucked-away little dale. Holidays were spent in the cottage at West Scrafton which he and Joan acquired in 1978. Here they escaped the crowds, spending much time walking with the dogs. Film sequences for *All Creatures Great and Small* were "shot" hereabouts.

Harrogate. Alf gave the celebrated spa town the fictitious name Brawton and, thinking of it as a haven from continuous hard work, he and Joan often visited the town on Thursday afternoons, when he had free time. They browsed in shops and had dainty meals in *Betty's Cafe*. For three decades they shared their limited time at Harrogate with Gordon Rae, the vet at Boroughbridge, and his wife Jean.

Leyburn. A market town in Wensleydale that became the base from which Alf assisted Frank Bingham, tuberculin-testing cattle, in a veterinary practice that introduced Alf to the upper dale-country, which he grew to love.

Pickering. A prominent house in Houndgate became the first fictitious Skeldale House.

Richmond. Alf and Joan went to the Zetland cinema at Richmond on their wedding day, breaking their journey to Carperby. Alf got to know Richmond well. To him, the historic, unspoilt old town was both

Thirsk – a busy town that was the base for Alf's veterinary work.

The distinctive clock tower in the centre of Thirsk.

charming and romantic.

Scarborough. Alf, though in a reserved occupation, volunteered for the R.A.F. early in the 1939-45 war, and was placed on deferred service, entering service in the autumn of 1942. Alf was stationed at the *Grand* during service with the R.A.F. Much later, he and Joan enjoyed day trips to the resort. In September, he was drawn to the town by the annual cricket festival.

Thirsk. A busy town with a cobbled market place, one of several parking areas for migrant motorists heading to or from the Moors and Coast. Thirsk was, of course, the base for Alf's veterinary work. He and Joan were married in the church. Alf was 25 and the bride 22. In due course, his children – Jimmy and Rosie – would be baptised and married there. In the summer of 2005, Emma Page, granddaughter of Alf, was married in this church to Joel Ward. The former home and surgery is now The Herriot Centre, open to the public at prescribed times.

Wensley. James and Helen Herriot were "married" at the local church in the television series *All Creatures Great and Small*.

West Witton. In Wensleydale, an early experience of Alf was recalled fictitiously when James descended Grassgill and Capple Bank in a brakeless car. He didn't arrive in the village of West Witton, having to turn the car into a roadside wall to avoid a flock of sheep!

York. Joan bought her wedding outfit here. Half-day holidays from the practice were spent in this historic city. And it was in the glorious Minster that a memorial service was held for Alf – a service attended by almost 2,000 people.

A Bibliography:

If Only They Could Talk (1970);
It Shouldn't Happen to a Vet (1972);
Let Sleeping Vets Lie (1973);
Vet in Harness (1974);
Vets Might Fly (1976);
Vet in a Spin (1977);
James Herriot's Yorkshire (1979);
The Lord God Made Them All (1981);
Every Living Thing (1992).

Omnibus Editions*:*

All Creatures Great and Small (1975), comprising *If Only They Could Talk* and *It Shouldn't Happen to a Vet.*
All Things Bright and Beautiful (1976), comprising *Let Sleeping Vets Lie* and *Vet in Harness.*
All Things Wise and Wonderful (1978), comprising *Vets Might Fly* and *Vet in a Spin.*

The Best of James Herriot (1982);
James Herriot's Dog Stories (1986);
James Herriot's Cat Stories (1994);
James Herriot's Favourite Dog Stories (1995);
James Herriot's Yorkshire Stories (1997).

Alf Wight wrote eight books for children.

Also by W.R. Mitchell, available from Great Northern Books:

HANNAH HAUXWELL – 80 Years in the Dales

The Official Biography to Celebrate the 80th Birthday of this Remarkable Dales Character
Hannah captured the hearts of the nation when she was the subject of an extraordinary
documentary, *Too Long a Winter*. The TV programme made her a national celebrity. Further
programmes followed. She went on tours of Europe and America, shook hands with the Pope and
played the piano on the Orient Express. This major book traces the extraordinary life of a delightful
personality who has never lost her links with the dales countryside.
Fully illustrated. Hardback.

"Hannah Hauxwell should be an inspiration to us all." Daily Mail

THUNDER IN THE MOUNTAINS – The Men Who Built Ribblehead

The harsh, often violent, true story of those who built Ribblehead Viaduct, is related in this
beautifully produced and fully illustrated hardback. For ten years, the railway settlement around
Batty Green was home to hundreds of navvies, their wives and children, who experienced
earthquake, flood and smallpox. Today, their monument is the landmark viaduct, carrying the much
loved, Settle-Carlisle line.
Fully illustrated. Hardback.

"… factual accuracy with racy story-telling" Yorkshire Post
"This true-life drama is gripping from start to finish." Patrick Stewart

WAINWRIGHT – His life from Milltown to Mountain

Bill Mitchell was a great friend of the legendary walker and writer, Alfred Wainwright. In this ground-
breaking, richly anecdotal and personal book about Wainwright, he recalls Wainwright's young days
in the Lancashire milltown of Blackburn and his fascination – as a lone walker – for wild places in
Lancashire, along the Pennines and in the north-west extremities of Scotland.
Fully illustrated. Hardback.

"I worked with AW on and off for five years but was still given a fresh glimpse of the great man in
this smashing new book"
Eric Robson Chairman, Wainwright Society

BEATRIX POTTER – Her Lakeland Years

The compelling story of the real Beatrix Potter, based on interviews with those who knew her.
Spread over the 40 years, these interviews recall memories stretching back to the time when Beatrix
bought the now famous Hill Top farm at Sawrey in the heart of Lakeland. She was already
internationally acclaimed for her series of 'Peter Rabbit' books and her local status was increased
when she married William Heelis, a Hawkshead solicitor. The books gave her the means to purchase
over 4,000 acres of land, which on her death in 1943 was bequeathed to the National Trust as her
personal legacy to the Lake District.
   The many archive and present-day photographs in this fully illustrated book place a new light on
the Lakeland years of Beatrix Potter.

Visit www.greatnorthernbooks.co.uk